ww

Dedicated to My Mom, Anna Pearsall
Who Worked in Customer Service
to Put Me Through School
PLUS She's An Avid Shopper & Customer!

Visit our website for more information as well as supplemental training, marketing and promotional materials.

www.customerserviceisfree.com

Notice:
Mention of specific companies and/or brand-name products in *Customer Service Is FREE* does not imply any endorsement by the publisher, author or the mentioned companies.

Customer Service Is FREE is a copyrighted book and cannot be reproduced. *Customer Service Is FREE* may be purchased for business or promotional use or for special sales. Custom printed editions are available with company logos on the cover or with a custom introduction. Specially priced quantity packages are available on our website as well as exclusive training tools (reference cards, bookmarks, posters) that can be printed with your business logo.

Copyright © 2010, 2011 by Customer Service Is FREE, LLC

All rights reserved. No part of this book may be reproduced or transmitted in any form or by any means, electronic or mechanical, including photocopying, recording, or by any information storage and retrieval system, without written permission from the publisher and author.

For information, please write to:

Customer Service Is FREE
P.O. Box 711
Lambertville, MI 48144

info@customerserviceisfree.com

ISBN-13: 978-0-9828321-0-3
ISBN-10: 0-9828321-0-9

Customer Service Is FREE!

WILLIAM T. PEARSALL

To-Do
- Learn 5 Customer Names ////
- ~~Schedule Focus Group~~
- **(Daily Customer Service Training Tip: SMILE)**
- ~~Share 5 Compliments~~ ////
- Print Customer Service Award
- ~~Return Phone Calls~~
- ~~Send Thank You Card~~
- ~~Respond to emails~~
- Say Hello to everyone!

Take A Number

The State of Customer Service	6
Smiles Are FREE	14
Greetings Are FREE	30
Recognition Is FREE	44
Manners Are FREE	58
Apologies Are FREE	68
Listening Is FREE	82
Appreciation Is FREE	96
The WOW Factor Is FREE	106
Attitudes Are FREE	116
Follow Through Is FREE	126
Communication Is FREE	136
Consistency Is FREE	146
Respect Is FREE	156
Compliments Are FREE	166
Honesty Is FREE	174
101 FREE Things You Can Do NOW	184
Summary	192

"I would complain about the customer service, but there wasn't any!"

~ Customers Everywhere

The State of Customer Service

It's difficult to believe that poor customer service is even tolerated. In many cases it's nonexistent and sometimes it's downright rude!

The state of customer service has deteriorated to a point that the public has become accepting of intolerable treatment and lack of care, concern or gratitude. People have become **desensitized** to bad customer service and the absence of common sense courtesies. It's just the way it is and there's nothing that can be done about it. Consumers feel that they have no choice, but to ...

Customer Service Is a CULTURE

- **Wait in long lines**
- **Be treated as a nuisance**
- **Settle for second best**

Sadly, it's rare to experience great service.

An endless parade of excuses is offered up by culpable businesses:

EXCUSES

- **Good employees are hard to find**
- **There is no money for training**
- **There is no time to spend on customer service**
- **The training department was downsized**
- **We don't need to improve customer service**
- **We can't hold the employees' hands**

The bottom line is, these are all excuses. It seems businesses are too eager to formulate reasons why service never gets better as opposed to just making it happen.

Businesses Can't Afford NOT to Spend Time on Customer Service

Customer service is immediate but it has **long term effects**, positive or negative, depending on the experience. Customer service is not rocket science. It's elementary and basic common sense. Plus, it's **FREE**!

Corporate America spends millions of dollars on marketing and promotion but often overlooks the importance of customer service. Companies fail to realize that they would be far more successful if they simply dedicated some time to improving customer service. They would get better results from **FREE** word-of-mouth advertising and repeat business than from one time print advertisements or bothersome television commercials.

Compare the Costs

30 Second Television Commercial	$100,000.00
One Month Billboard Advertisement	$20,000.00
10,000 Piece Direct Mailing Advertisement	$5,000.00
Full Page Newspaper Ad	$2,000.00

Excellent Customer Service   FREE

The **ultimate** goal of customer service is to ensure that customers are satisfied and happy. Satisfied customers will not only return and spend more money, but they will also become ambassadors of the business, promoting it and raving to family and friends about the superior service.

Everyone knows what customer service is. Everyone also knows that customer service today is **terrible**. What happened to excellent service?

Customers Are The #1 Priority

Excellence in customer service starts at the top. You've taken a step in the right direction simply by reading this book. You realize that there's room for improvement and it shows that you are genuinely concerned about customer satisfaction. This book is your guide to great customer service across the board.

Customer Service Is About People

1. How **people** are treated
2. Whether or not **people** are happy
3. If **people** provide great service
4. How **people** project the image of a business
5. Whether or not **people** care

Customer service not only involves the interaction of employees with customers, but also the importance of interactions and communication between employees and their superiors. Effective customer service requires placing the right people, with the **right attitudes**, in key interactive positions.

You Have to Make the Commitment

Pledge to do something **every day** to advance the quality of service in your establishment. That commitment will be the best investment that you could ever make.

Any business can offer the best product at a great value, but they will miss the mark if they fail to deliver consistent service.

Show Your Customers How Valuable they Are to You

Start today!

You don't need elaborate action plans, budget approvals, more hours in a day or even money. Simply make it a priority to devote a small portion of time *every day* to improving the quality of customer service. Train excellent customer service principles NOW!

Persistence pays.
Customer service does too!

I implore everyone, not only as business owners and managers, but also as consumers, to patronize, and recommend businesses that provide superior service. As customers continue to expect excellent customer service, it will get better as a whole. The sole fact that one business gets better will cause others to get better as well. It's a continuous cycle of improvement.

Consumers Speak with Their Pocketbooks!

Businesses today are **fighting for customers**. Failing to make the commitment to improve customer service on a daily basis could cost you customers and your business, literally. If you don't make the commitment, someone else will.

A Little Effort Goes a Long Way

My goal in writing this book is to show you that if you dedicate the time and the effort toward increasing the quality of customer service you will reap the rewards. From years of experience as a customer service manager, certified corporate trainer, business owner and, most importantly, a **consumer** I have come to realize that excellent customer service is the driving force behind all successful businesses.

Constantly Strive to Improve Customer Service

This book presents everyday principles, practical exercises, ideals and realistic tools to help you take your customer service to the next level.

Making the Most of Customer Service Is FREE

Customer Service Is FREE is **loaded** with useful information to aid you in your journey to excellence. You will find exercises, worksheets, checklists and more. I recommend that you have a highlighter, pen and paper handy so you can note important and helpful information. Dog ear the pages that you want to refer back to or leave sticky notes by crucial topics.

■■■■■■■■■■■■■■■■■■■■■■■■■■■■■

There Is Always Room for Improvement

■■■■■■■■■■■■■■■■■■■■■■■■■■■■■

This book is a **quick read**. Keep it on your desk as a reminder of the importance of customer service.

The chapters are not listed in any particular order. When you look at the big picture that is the customer experience, every aspect is equally as important as the next.

Implement the tools and methods you learn. Incorporate *Customer Service Is FREE* into your cus-

---

A Customer by Any Other Name ...

Guest • Patient • Client • Patron • Buyer
Shopper • Prospect • Consumer • Purchaser

... Would Still Want Great Service!

www.customerserviceisfree.com

Who Can Benefit from Reading?

- CEOs
- Owners
- Trainers
- Cashiers
- Waiters
- Greeters
- Nurses
- Managers
- Supervisors
- Training Directors
- Receptionists
- Sales People
- Bell Hops
- Janitors

Anyone that Interacts with Customers!

tomer service training at all levels. Although it's written for owners and management, anyone, at any level, will benefit from the content.

Check out the *Customer Service Is FREE* companion website, **www.customerserviceisfree.com**. You'll find additional information, interactive forums, customer service tips, personal anecdotes, printable training forms, signs, posters, awards and assessments and even a **FREE** monthly newsletter. Register online to gain access to the exclusive areas of the website.

Good luck on your journey to excellent customer service.

is a great place to start!

Customer Service Is FREE

"A smile is something you can't give away; it always comes back to you."

~Author Unknown

Smiles Are FREE!

Let's start with a simple exercise. Close your eyes and force yourself to smile for 30 seconds.

What happened? Did you think about things that made you smile? Your children? A joke? Relaxing on a beach in Tahiti? How could you *not* think of something that makes you smile when you closed your eyes and **forced** yourself to smile?

If nothing else you smiled because of how funny you must look while sitting there smiling!

What Makes You SMILE?

The act of smiling forces you to think positive, good, happy and sometimes ridiculous thoughts.

Customer Service Starts with a SMILE

EXERCISE

The opening Smile Starter Exercise is great to use at any point in time whether you are alone or with others, at work or at home. It works every time and will help to focus your thoughts on positives and away from negatives that might be floating around your mind. Customer service employees should start every shift with a quick smiling exercise.

As simple as it may seem, smiling is also the perfect way to start customer service meetings and training sessions. Try this exercise to get everyone's attention: Walk into the room. Don't talk. Walk around and smile at people while making eye contact with them. Smile at as many people as you can. What was the result? What did people do in return? They smiled back!

Most Smiles Are Started by Another Smile

A smile accomplished all that without even a word! It **drives the point** home and breaks the ice. In group settings, be sure to take some time to discuss what made people smile. Spend some time and really delve into what these thoughts conjure up in your minds.

Why do these positive, happy thoughts make people smile? Consider the end results and the overwhelming significance these thoughts have in making us smile.

- ▶ Warm
- ▶ Happy
- ▶ Pleasing
- ▶ Comforting
- ▶ Welcoming
- ▶ Contagious

There are so many positives to smiling that it is really the best place to start discussing customer service. That's why I chose to start this book with smiles.

Smiles Are the BEST *Positive Perception*

When someone smiles at you it's a natural impulse to smile back. Plus smiles are **FREE**! You can spend **hundreds & thousands of dollars** on customer service training programs, books, seminars, research and more, but if you don't have smiling faces you might as well pour your money down the drain.

Say "**Cheese!**"

That phrase creates positive **perceptions** in photographs. It forces people to appear as if they are smiling. It gives the perception that they are happy. That's how everyone wants to be remembered, happy and smiling. No one wants to be photographed in their class picture or wedding portrait with a frown. When you look at a person that is smiling it is assumed that the person is happy. *That's* what we want to preserve and remember.

Smiling Is the Most Basic, Core Concept of Service

We've all heard "Service with a smile!" Everyone knows it but how often does it actually happen? Have you ever gone to a retail store where the cashier never cracked a smile once? What did you think about that person? Did they have any desire to make your experience of spending money

Share Your Smiles

a pleasant one? You would have gotten more smiles if you went through the self checkout!

Share your smiles. Your smile is the best, priceless, **first impression** that you could possibly offer to anyone, in any business, whether you're a cashier at a store, a hostess at a restaurant or an usher at a theater. Smiles are inviting and they convey friendliness, happiness and gratitude.

■■■■■■■■■■■■■■■■■■■■■■■■■■■■■■■

Put on a Happy Face
You Only Get One Chance to Make that First Impression

■■■■■■■■■■■■■■■■■■■■■■■■■■■■■■■

Everyone understands smiles whether you speak Swahili or English and whether you are 2 or 82. It's an expression that is **understood by everyone**.

I can count on one hand the number of times that I have seen an employee smiling in a discount retail store. It makes me want to leave!

Everyone Has Smiles

It's so rare to see smiles in service that it's a wonder people truly remember how to smile. That scary thought sums up the quality of service in today's market. **There's much more to be desired.**

As a customer, you encounter employees that are not smiling on a regular basis. You immediately assume that the employee is unhappy and most likely

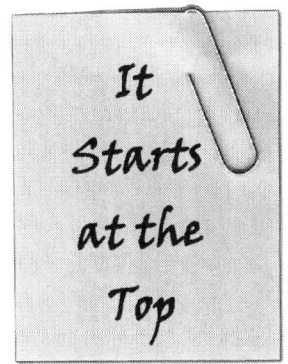

It Starts at the Top

Happy Managers Attract Happy Customer Service Professionals

not enjoying the time they are assisting you. That also translates into the fact that the employee's work environment is not a pleasant one, otherwise they would be happy and smiling.

Frowning Employees Just Go Through the Motions to Get a Paycheck

Frowners have no ownership or passion in what they are doing, whether it be a sales person, a greeter or even a telephone operator.

Employers **must** give their customer service staff something to smile about, teach them the significance of smiling and how it benefits them.

Employees Represent Companies

Customer service professionals work the front lines and directly represent the business to the public. If they feel threatened, stressed and frustrated they are not going to smile. You can't have a successful business full of employees that are walking on egg shells because they aren't sure what is going to set the boss off next.

These employees are going to be preoccupied with thoughts of leaving and finding another job that offers a fun, comfortable working atmosphere where the boss smiles too.

Managers must always remember that employees are their "**customers**" and they deserve great customer service from their superiors. Managers should lead by example and offer smiles just as a they would expect of the customer service professionals they employ.

Smiles Put People at Ease

A supervisor's smile makes him or her approachable. It helps them to maintain an **open door policy** where the service staff can feel at ease coming to them with service issues.

Here's a simple management exercise that takes very little time and can be done every day.

Daily Smile Exercise

At the start of your day make it a point to approach each and every employee, **SMILE** and greet them by name.

Hello, Mike!

This daily exercise shows that management is happy and really cares. It gets everyone off on the right foot.

Some people are simply not smilers. You may need to teach the **non-smilers** to look happy when they are interacting with customers, guests and employees. It's something that they have to focus on and continually remember to do.

Smiles Are Imperative to Customer Service

If you encounter people in the workplace that are not smiley you have to find ways to make them smile. Talk to them about it, they might not even be aware that they don't smile. Often times people get so focused on the work at hand that they appear angry and stern. They simply need a **trigger** to bring their smile back.

SMILE TRIGGERS

- Jokes
- Images of Loved Ones
- Pets
- A Particular Song
- Vacation Spots
- A Room Full Of Naked People
- A Cartoon
- A Character from a Sitcom or Movie
- Your Dream Date
- A Funny Word
- Clowns
- ***Anything*** That Makes You Smile

Take a few moments and make a list of your own triggers, the things that make you smile. Hang on to that piece of paper so you can refer to it later.

Turn that Frown Upside Down

A friend that I worked with would force a goofy smile every time she walked by me when I wasn't smiling. This, in turn, forced me to smile back and to be conscious of the fact that I was not smiling. That was my **smile trigger**. It sounds silly but it worked. It was a non verbal form of "turn that frown upside down." Friends, coworkers or even your boss can be great motivators to smile.

Smile triggers create genuine smiles, real smiles. They are not forced or fake. They look sincere. It is not the obviously, uncomfortable smile that you project when you are smiling for the sake of smiling. You want to smile because you are truly happy and thinking happy thoughts. People can see right through a forced smile. Be sure that your smile triggers are **genuine**.

Know Your Smile Triggers

Plan of Action: Remove non-smilers from your front lines. Move them to a different position where they don't have direct contact with your patrons. You may seriously even need to consider letting a non-smiler go if you have unsuccessfully attempted to work with them to bring out their smiles. If it comes to this remember that you can point it out and tell them every day, but it is ultimately their decision to smile or not.

Smiling is one of the key deciding factors that I would recommend using when interviewing potential customer service employees. If you go through an entire interview and the interviewee doesn't crack a smile, Make it a point not to hire that person.

Consider your current staff. Divide them into two lists, smilers and frowners. Are there people that never smile? Evaluate why the frowners aren't smiling. Are they unhappy with their job? Are they aware they aren't smiling?

❓ Does Your Staff Smile ❓

The **bottom line** is you have to get the frowners to move to the smilers list! Frowning is just as (if not more) contagious as smiling. The frowns and the attitudes that are associated with them can break down the morale of your staff and have a direct impact on customer service. It requires immediate attention.

People that Smile Are Attractive

Do you know someone that always smiles? Is that person crazy? You can't help but smile back and wonder what's going on in their head.

I would be willing to bet it is simply because they are happy and content with their life. Spend time around that person. Their smile is contagious and **will** wear off on you.

Smiles make your face **light up** and **radiate** the joy that you have within you. Smiling can actually be seen in your eyes. Your eyes literally widen and beam, evidence that smiles are generated from your spirit and soul.

Smile with Eye Contact

Furthermore, as you speak while you smile, the tone of your voice is audibly different. You sound sincere and pleasant. It is uplifting, soothing and calming. The words simply flow more graciously and it is apparent, even when you are speaking to someone that you cannot see. This is why it's important to smile even when you're on the telephone. The caller will be able to "hear" your smile!

SMILING
Can Change the Way You Do Business

Smiling is so important to customers that it can literally **change** the way you do business and who you do business with. For example, I buy gas at a gas station that charges more than any other gas station around. Why? It's because the people that work there are always smiling and making me feel welcome. I would rather spend the extra money and know that my sale is appreciated and that the staff is happy. I don't want to start my morning off with grouchy people taking my money. Who would? **Smiles are contagious** and I want them wherever I can get them.

A Smiling Person Is a Happy Person

It is easier to approach a smiling person. A smile is welcoming and serves as an invitation. When you look at the big picture you are more willing to pay a premium for excellent service from smiling and happy people.

A customer service staff that does not smile makes customers feel **uncomfortable**! It's as if you are a nuisance and you are intruding on their bad mood. You don't want to approach that person. It's awkward and, quite frankly, rude. Imagine if you are in a place that has many employees, none of which are smiling. How quickly would you want to leave?

On the other hand, think of the places that do have smiling, happy employees. You want to stay because you feel welcome and comfortable. You want to open your wallet and spend your money there!

This is the Lure of Smiling

- Happy Customers
- Happy Employees
- Higher Customer Satisfaction
- Higher Sales

Million Dollar Smiles Are *Priceless*

Smile Exercises

1 Smile Starter

Close your eyes and force yourself to smile. Do this for 30 seconds. This simple exercise focuses positive thoughts and generates smiles.

2 Group Smile Starter

Make an unannounced entrance. Don't talk. Smile at people and make direct eye contact. Start a meeting after this quick exercise now that you have everyone's *happy* attention!

3 Manager Smile Starter

At the start of each shift approach every employee, smile and greet them. Do this *daily* and you will see an instant change in attitude.

4 Smile Triggers

Write down a list of things, ideas, people and events that make you smile. Use this list as your guide to smiling. Carry this list with you for reference.

5 Smile Evaluations

Divide your employees into groups of smilers and frowners. Through training, turn frowners into smilers. Re-evaluate often until there are no frowners.

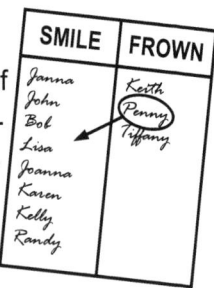

6 Phone Smiles

Smiles can be heard through the telephone. Practice smiling when you speak on the phone and you will notice that you sound and feel better.

www.customerserviceisfree.com

Throughout *Customer Service Is FREE* you will find relevant award certificates. Awards are powerful forms of recognition and reinforce customer service values.

Find a **FREE** printable version of this Smile Award on our website, www.customerserviceisfree.com.

Customer Service Is FREE

Greetings Go Hand-In-Hand with Smiles

Greetings Are FREE!

Take a moment to put yourself in your customer's shoes. Visualize walking into your store or business. Are you greeted? Do you encounter an employee? Is it warm, welcoming and inviting? Are you offered a smile?

A Smile Is a Universal Greeting

No matter what language you speak the combination of a smile and a greeting create the most important part of any customer service experience, **the first impression**. First impressions can make or break the entire experience. If you start off on the wrong foot you may not get another chance to overcome a less than stellar greeting.

Many companies believe so **strongly** (rightly so) in greetings that they have employees stationed near the entrance. Restaurants place hostesses near the entrance so that customers are greeted **immediately**. Hotels have door men. Business and medical settings have receptionists and many retailers have greeters that open doors and welcome guests as they enter.

The People Greeter

Wal-Mart, the world's largest retailer, wants you to start your experience in their store with a warm greeting as well. In fact, they have created an employee position to make sure of it. This person's title is aptly named, the **People Greeter**. The typical greeter's job responsibilities include welcoming patrons with eye contact, charisma and a smile. They also serve as directors and point customers in the right direction. Furthermore, greeters make customers feel valuable.

Here's a reality check:

Every person in a place of business should be considered a greeter!

Greetings go beyond the entrance. If any employee comes into contact with a customer they should offer a smile and a greeting. A simple "good afternoon" would be perfect.

During a stay at a historic hotel I encountered such a situation. Every *single* employee in the resort, from the house keepers, to the door men, to the landscapers, smiled and expressed some greeting. That was over 10 years ago and I still remember it. It made a lasting impression.

Ideally, each greeter's responsibility is to greet customers (among other tasks), but they often fall short of this simple task. Don't get me wrong, people go through the motions and speak the words, but they are not **passionate**, **emotional** or **convincing**. Often, in busy settings, greetings are blurted out without ever thinking. The repetition sounds **insincere and mindless**. To combat this problem, vary greetings and avoid the ever rehearsed "Welcome to ..."

Greetings Can Sound Robotic

Personalize Greetings

An easy way to create unique and **memorable** greetings is to offer a sincere compliment to the customer. Tell them that you love their coat or jewelry, that their children are well behaved or that it is a pleasure to see them. Everyone loves and remembers a compliment.

A standard greeting that I routinely hear from restaurant hostesses is "Two tonight?" It is stated matter-of-factly, in a monotone voice, without smiling, sincerity or even a remote tinge of concern about welcoming customers from the podium they hide behind.

Greeters Set the Course

These greetings set restaurants up for **failure** by setting the bar very low and failing to deliver a memorable first impression. The impression given is that the dining event will be lifeless, just like the greeting. So, you see, the experience is poor before it really even begins.

The most **memorable greeting** that I can recall was after a very long, tiring flight. I walked off the plane and down the exit ramp to a beautiful, smiling woman in a grass skirt offering me a flowered lei and a heartfelt greeting.

Aloha! Welcome to Hawaii!

From that moment on, I knew that my visit was going to be unique, friendly and **cultural**. My first impression of Hawaii was, "Wow! This is a great place to be!" I was so impressed that I told everyone I know. It was a truly memorable experience.

Everything About That Greeting Was Perfect

The Hawaiian girl was beaming from ear to ear with a warm, inviting smile. She was sincere and offered a greeting that was different and unforgettable. Furthermore, her cheerful disposition **set the tone** for the rest of the Hawaiian experience. I couldn't help but return the smile and thank her. She introduced me to her island home with joy and happiness. Her smile and greeting makes me want to return to Hawaii and her sincerity makes me want to stay!

Sincere Greetings Are Critical

Important Points to Consider

- Greeters should be **aware**, focused & attentive to the needs of customers.

- Greetings should be **immediate** and direct.

- As soon as **eye contact** is made, the greeter should offer a verbal greeting.

- Greeters should **speak first** in order to control the conversation.

A customer should **never** have to wait to be greeted while an employee finishes a conversation with another employee.

Employees Must Be Trained Not To Congregate

When employees stand in groups they are focused on their conversation and not on the needs of the customer or the best interest of the business.

Something to Talk About

Discuss the perfect greeting for your business.

What is said?

When should it happen?

Who do you want to be your first point of contact?

I recently walked into a store where there was a group of employees socially chatting. I had a

Put Conversations on Hold to Greet Customers

question but could not get their attention. Obviously, their conversation was far more important than me. They were not aware of my needs. They made no attempt to greet me, let alone acknowledge me. I even had to walk around them! What kind of greeting is that?

If a greeter is involved in a conversation when a customer approaches, **eye contact** should be made with them and the conversation should be wrapped up quickly. Direct eye contact assures the customer that their presence is known. In situations when a customer does have to wait for a greeter to finish with another customer, a quick apology should be offered prior to the greeting:

"Thank you for your patience."

When customers are waiting in a line, acknowledgement is beneficial. A simple, "We'll be right with you, ma'am," conveys awareness and a sense of urgency that they'll be taken care of as quickly as possible. This simple acknowledgement and greeting creates the appearance of organization and awareness from the greeter.

Appearances Are Everything

Greeters must look representative of the business that they are **ambassadors** for. Greeters should be kempt, well groomed and dressed appropriately.

If there is a dress code or uniform it should be clean and fresh. In business settings a suit is appropriate, however in a doctor's office, medical scrubs would fit the bill. The **bottom line** is, the greeter's appearance speaks volumes about the business without saying a word. Moreover, smiles should be a part of every greeter's dress code. I would recommend changing any greeter's written dress code to include smiles. **It's that important!**

Knowledgeable Greeters Are Essential

10 Components of a GREAT Greeting

1 • SMILE

2 • Eye Contact

3 • Sincerity/Conviction

4 • Appearance

5 • Verbalization

6 • Attention/Awareness/Focus

7 • Urgency

8 • Charisma

9 • Professional & Knowledgeable

10 • Memorable

Greeters are the **first point of contact** and should be able to answer any customer's question. They should also be able to direct customers, provide information and share expertise about the business. Place informed people in greeter positions to ensure a positive first impression.

Think about your home. What's the first impression that you make on a guest when they visit? It's always a warm, friendly, welcoming "Hello!" You open the door to greet them with open arms and a smile! Recreate this personal greeting for your customers to experience. Open the door for customers when you can and invite them into your business. Customers should feel that you *truly* want them to be there. Do this in all business environments. Get up from your chair, invite clients in, shake their hands.

Handshakes Are Free Too

Handshakes are not appropriate in every setting, but for sales and business environments they are **perfect**. Handshakes are appropriate for women as well. The physical aspect of a handshake reinforces the greeting and makes a special connection of trust, confidence and sincerity.

Avoid the weak, limp fish and the overpowering vice-grip handshakes. Find a happy medium. A simple, firm, confident shake that says "Glad to see you," will suffice.

A Proper Handshake

1. Make eye contact
2. Smile
3. Offer your right hand
4. Firmly grasp the customer's hand in your palm with your thumbs parallel to each other & your fingers wrapped snugly around the bottom of their hand
5. Shake in a quick, short, up and down motion 2 - 3 times, then release your firm grip

Are your greeters making a lasting impression? Remember that list of smilers and frowners that you made in the last chapter? Take another look. What side are your greeters on?

By now, you should certainly come to the conclusion that it is **mandatory** that your greeters be on the smilers list. These are the people that are representing your business and everything that it stands for. Be sure that they are portraying happiness through a warm, professional and inviting greeting.

First Impressions & Memorable Greetings Set You Up For Success

Greetings to Avoid

1 ✦ The Non-Greeting - Someone is there but offers no greeting whatsoever

2 ✦ The Robot - Repeats the same greeting to every customer

3 ✦ The Deadpan - Expressionless face, no smiles

4 ✦ Over the Top - Enough already, turn it down a notch, not convincing

5 ✦ The Greeting Whisperer - Speaks so softly you can't even hear

6 ✦ The Preoccupied - Too busy talking to coworkers or on the phone

7 ✦ The Invisible - What greeter? There's no one around!

8 ✦ Speed Racer - Speaks so quickly you can't keep up or understand what they said

9 ✦ The Hidden - Hides behind a podium, desk or other object

10 ✦ The Fake Out - Is obviously acting, not sincere in the least

Do Your Homework! International Greetings

If you are traveling to another country, representing your company, you are serving as an international greeter. Greeting people from other cultures requires a little pre-greet research to understand the appropriate form of greeting. The etiquette may include a bow, a kiss on the hand, a nod of the head or some other gesture or phrase.

Some gestures or phrases might be considered insulting. Foreign customers will be pleasantly surprised and will most certainly remember your greeting if you take the time and interest to learn what their traditions are. It could be the lasting impression that makes the sale!

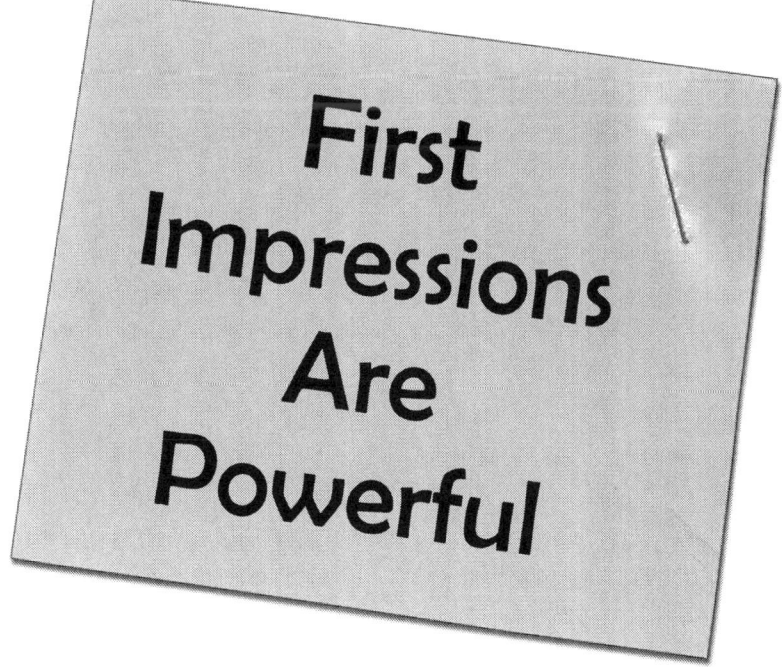

First Impressions

You only have one chance to make a first impression. Do you know what kind of impression your business and employees are making?

As you approach a business the exterior projects an impression. It should be clean, orderly and well kept. It sends a subliminal message: **this business cares about quality**, but, most importantly, the quality of service and the quality of the products they sell.

■■■■■■■■■■■■■■■■■■■■■■■■■■■■

You Never Get A Second Chance To Make A First Impression

■■■■■■■■■■■■■■■■■■■■■■■■■■■■

Theme parks are great with first impressions. They are always **impeccably** landscaped with brightly colored, ornate flowers. There's nearly always an employee with a broom and dustpan picking up any trace of trash. It screams fun, tidy and organized. It's welcoming. It says "Get ready for a great time!"

Imagine walking up to that same theme park in this scenario: trash is blowing across the sidewalk, employees are smoking outside the entrance gate and the shrubs are dead, overcome with weeds.

Are you still thinking **fun**? Do you feel that they maintain their park rides? Do you want to take that risk?

Apply these same principles to your business. Imagine a warm, heartfelt greeting from a well groomed greeter accompanied by a smile that is welcoming and friendly. Set your customers up to have a great customer service experience. Create a first impression that is positive, professional and long-lasting.

Greet Your Customers with Open Arms

First Impressions can invite customers in or send them away to the competition. Good or bad, they are **FREE**. They can be **priceless** or **costly**. The choice is yours.

First Impression Malfunctions

- ▶ No Smiles
- ▶ No Greeting
- ▶ Trash
- ▶ Slouching
- ▶ Dirty Uniforms
- ▶ No Employee In Sight
- ▶ Smoking Employees
- ▶ Poor Maintenance
- ▶ Chewing Gum
- ▶ Personal Conversations

What's In a Name?

A **Wealth** of Business, of Course!

Recognition Is FREE!

NOW SERVING 3

Whether it's retail, manufacturing or hospitality, every business has their repeat or regular customers. These valuable customers are the ones that the staff recognizes instantly. They learn what regulars like and dislike, what their needs are, the way business has to be conducted with them and most importantly, their names!

Regular Customers Are the **Backbone** of Any Business

Customers are remembered simply because of the fact that they spend a significant amount of time and money with the establishment. Regular customers are **loyal** promoters of any business. The word-of-mouth advertising they offer colleagues, family and friends is **priceless**! You couldn't pay for promotion of this caliber from better ambassadors.

Learn Customers' Names

Your goal should be to learn **all** customers' names and turn them into repeat customers. When you see customers that you recognize and you don't know their names, you must make it a point to turn them into known regulars.

Look for indicators that customers are new to your establishment:

♦ Are customers looking for the restrooms, service counter, or cashier?
♦ Are they searching for certain products?
♦ Do they seem confused?

These hints should clue you in to the fact that the person is not a regular and offers a **prime** opportunity to learn who that person is. Go out of your way to learn their name. The goal is to make customers know that they are so important to your business that you want to remember who they are.

Much like employees want to be recognized for their achievements, customers want to be recognized for their patronage. Customers want to feel appreciated, important, and significant.

If the customer service staff is taught to learn and use the names of clientele and verbally recognize them, the number of repeat customers will continue to grow.

Imagine the results if you were able to recognize *all* of your customers and use their names. You would turn people into **lifetime,** invaluable, repeat business partners and friends. The sales and promotional impact is endless. The sky's the limit!

From a customer's point of view recognition is a form of respect, respect from the establishment that they are appreciative of the business. Along with this respect comes common manners and courtesy. Address customers with proper form and etiquette. Use titles and full names unless instructed otherwise. Don't ever assume that it is appropriate to use a common nickname or shortened version of a name.

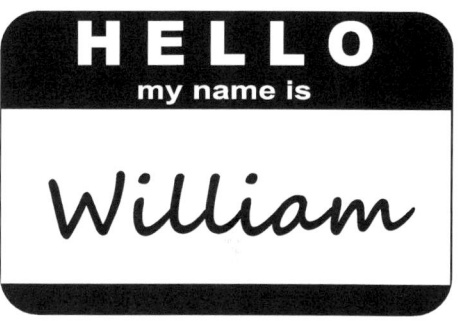

Not Will, Willie or Bill

Service staff should be taught to learn and use customers' names whenever they can. If a customer's name is known then it should be shared and used by everyone. If a customer's name is not known then attempts should be made to learn it. You can discretely learn names from credit cards, reservations or other documentation.

Introduce Yourself

Let the customer know that you recognize them, would like to know what their name is and that you appreciate their continued business.

There are many ways to learn customers' names. Finding out what's best for you and your employees may take practice.

Try these methods and exercises with your customer service staff and spark some enthusiasm.

1 Associate Your Associates

Associate the person's name with something familiar or comical. For example: John Applebaum - think Johnny Appleseed, or Apple Butter.

The association could be as simple as relating the person to someone else that you know that happens to share the same or a similar name or remembering something unique about the person such as a particularly different hairstyle.

Animal associations are helpful because they are lighthearted. For example: Mrs. Jones' hair looked like a poodle's. Mr. Johnson is as stubborn as a mule.

There are other simple associations that will work as well. What car does the customer drive? Does the customer have a distinctive voice? Do they have an accent?

2 Get It Write!

Writing their name down works wonders. It can be on a scrap piece of paper, on a pad that lists names of repeat customers or on index cards in a file that lists other information about the person like family members' names, place of employment, etc. If you use this method you should take a few uninterrupted moments to review your list at the end of the day to help reinforce your memory.

Share It!

Once you know a name, share the name with coworkers who can help you remember it. Your coworkers can then use the name too!

Shake It Out of Them!

Offer your name, a smile and a handshake. The person will surely offer the same!

Repetition, Repetition, Repetition

Once you learn a new name use it immediately. For example: "Mr. Walton, great to meet you. It's nice to finally put a name with the face after all these years. Let me know if I can help you in the future. Have a great day Mr. Walton, take care." It's helpful to repeat the name silently to yourself after the conversation to continue reinforcing it. Continued repetition is particularly beneficial with difficult names.

It's All on Their Card

Ask professionals for one of their business cards. They contain a wealth of information that includes their address, telephone number and title. The business card will also allow you the opportunity to associate the customer's name with their business (i.e. personal trainer, stock broker, etc.). Use the back of the card to jot down other important information such as family members' names, preferences, significant dates

Customer Service Is FREE
William T. Pearsall
Customer Service Consultant
www.customerserviceisfree.com

(birthdays, anniversaries). Once you have the contact info, **try this** for a memorable impression - send a short note by e-mail or regular mail, letting the customer know that it was a pleasure meeting them and you hope to see them again soon.

Now, That's Great Customer Service!

7 🛑 Stop, Look & Remember

When you meet someone give them your undivided attention. Focus on the person, their **features**, their **voice**, their **demeanor**, their **personality**. Look at them, **really look at them**. Make eye contact with the person and truly recognize everything that you can for future reference. Find something about this person that is unique that will help you recall them the next time you see them.

8 Get to Know Them

While conversing with the customer learn something about them personally. For example, they own a Yorkshire Terrier named Bella or their son plays little league for the local elementary school or the customer loves to travel to Europe. Often times personal information will stick in your mind. Make a simple association of this information with their name.

Use these methods to learn new names **every day**. Learn them. Use them. Even if you are not directly assisting this customer, go out of your way to greet them with a welcoming smile and a heartfelt hello. "Good afternoon Mr. Wright, great to see you again!" Trust me, Mr. Wright will be impressed that you said anything, let alone remembered his name.

Names Put You on Friendly Terms with Your Customers

Recognition and use of names personalizes the situation and makes customers feel at ease and comfortable in your presence. It's like welcoming them into your home. They are family. If your product or service is mediocre, but the customer feels personally attached to your business, they will often overlook faults because of the personal connection. They will be more understanding and forgiving.

Personalize the Experience

The King Theory

It really is quite impressive when you go to a business where they know your name and what you like. It strokes the ego a bit and makes the you feel like you are the

King of the Domain!

Personalizing the experience also plays a huge role when your regulars are in the presence of others, whether it be family members, business clients, other customers or strangers

Recognition Makes People Feel Important & Appreciated

Dr. Smith goes to a particular restaurant that he calls his favorite. When he arrives the smiling hostess greets him by name, "Good evening Dr. Smith. We have your usual booth available for you and your server, Mary, is getting your favorite martini as we speak!" It is quite obvious to the other patrons that Dr. Smith is known at his favorite restaurant.

Upon being seated at his favorite table, Mary approaches the table with Dr. Smith's martini in-hand, "Great to see you Dr. Smith! Here's your martini, extra dry with anchovy olives and a twist, just how you like it." Dr. Smith feels important and distinguished. Just imagine how Dr. Smith would feel if he were accompanied by some business partners. He would certainly **feel like a king**!

Use Caution with Recognition

You don't want *any* customer, especially those that could turn into regular customers, to feel slighted because you are spending too much time with the regulars. New customers want to know why the regular customers gets all the attention? Therefore, you must make it a point to spend time with *new* customers so you can learn and use their names as well. Use the previously mentioned methods to learn new customers' names while you are chatting with them and make them feel at home. Be sure to thank them and invite them back.

Make Every Customer Feel Like They Are Getting "Special Treatment"

Challenged or problem situations offer a unique opportunity to recognize customers. Addressing these situations places you in direct contact with potential regulars. Turn these situations into positive situations by learning their names and turning the people into repeat customers. Follow through with them and make a lasting impression.

These patrons often become your best regular customers once you successfully resolve the issue. They will become your most **loyal supporters**.

Nurture Customers into Regulars

Customer recognition will be one of the most important customer service techniques that you can pursue. It will have life-long impact. Many businesses are lucky enough to cultivate and serve generations of regulars. The financial investment is zero and the financial impact is **priceless**.

It's Serious Business

It also costs nothing to recognize **employees** that excel in customer recognition. In fact, employee recognition is crucial in any quest to learn and use customers' names. This refers not only to employee recognition for practical and daily use of customers' names but also to general employee recognition for positive behavior and performance not related to customer recognition.

Don't Forget Employee Recognition

If employees are recognized and happy, they will, in turn, provide **better service** and take the time to learn and use customers' names. Recognize employees for excellent customer recognition and other accomplishments. Give incentives and awards for learning, using and sharing customers' names. Employee recognition often gets overlooked and is a very worthwhile investment in your business, whatever it may be.

It starts at the top!
If management recognizes customers, the customer service staff will as well.

www.customerserviceisfree.com

Presenting awards is an incredible, **FREE** way to boost morale and improve customer service. Take advantage of the awards throughout *Customer Service Is FREE*. Reap the reward of improved customer service through employee recognition.

Find a **FREE** printable version of this Recognition Award on our website, www.customerserviceisfree.com.

Cash In On The POWER & Value Of Recognition

Exercises in Learning Names

1 ✦ Group Your Thoughts -
With a group of employees list ten names of regulars that are prominent in your business. Share ways of remembering these vital customers and make sure that the employees know who they are and use their names in the future. This would be a great weekly task, always learning and sharing 10 new names. Your customers will notice! For example, Mrs. Brown is the elderly lady that comes in every Tuesday when we do mark downs. She's here at 10am sharp right as we unlock the doors. Everyone must greet Mrs. Brown by name every Tuesday from here on out! Mrs. Brown will be thrilled!

2 ✦ Put Yourself in the Customer's Shoes -
Where do you go that you are considered a regular? What do you like about being a regular there? How are you recognized? Do they use your name? List the reasons that you are a regular customer and be sure to enforce them in your daily routine.

3 ✦ List Them for All to See -
Use a chalk board or easel pad to write down names as you see the regular customers so that the customer service staff is aware that they are in the house. Start a regular board or some other informal way to share who your regular customers are. Do this in a place that is highly visible to the staff for maximum exposure and shared knowledge.

4 ✦ Make a Game of It -
See who can list the most regulars or see who recognizes the most people in a particular time frame or shift. Offer incentives for learning, using and sharing names.

Please.
Thank You.
Ma'am.
My Goodness!

Manners Are FREE!

Everyone knows when to say "Thank you" and to say "Pardon me" if you walk in front of someone. Certainly, everyone knows that you respectfully address a gentleman with "sir." We are **taught** this from a very early age. We are also taught to hold doors open, to let ladies go first and to not interrupt.

What Happened to Manners?

How many service professionals actually practice these most elementary of manners?

Manners are fundamental to service and as direct as a child's education. They are trainable behavior.

It Takes
► Observation
► Patience
► Persistence

You can't truly know what your service staff is, or is not, saying or doing. You must observe and listen to them as they interact with your customers.

You can, however, get some good indicators from routine conversations.

Start With The Interview

If an interviewee does not show basic respect in the interview, they are less likely to show it in day to day behavior. Did the prospective employee thank you for your time? Shake your hand? Show decorum?

The BIG 4

- Please
- Thank You
- Excuse Me
- You're Welcome

Think about this and evaluate your current customer service staff. Do they use manners when they interact with you, your management team, or co-workers? Do they show basic respect? If they don't, they probably don't show it with customers either. It's something to keep an eye on.

Somewhere along the way, in our hustle and bustle life, we often overlook the common respect of daily manners and courtesy. On a daily basis I encounter customer service personnel that forget even basic courtesies and what socially correct behavior is. Often I'm lucky if I get a word or two out of the employee, let alone *please,* *thank you* and *you're welcome*!

Manners Are a Simple Display of Respect

Manners translate into **gratitude** for people (and customers) around you. Proper etiquette shows that you care enough about the situations, conversations, people and relationships that you experience every day, that you want to be respectful and gracious with them.

Manners Show Appreciation

You want your customers to know that you are thankful and that you realize that they are what your business is all about. Customers make your business survive and thrive. Be sure that they know that they are appreciated by being respectful and using your best manners.

Manners Beget Manners

When you use manners and show respect you ultimately get them right back from both customers and employees. Manners make your daily conversations and interactions more **enjoyable**. If you give appreciation, you will be appreciated.

Mind Your Manners

Ladies First

Don't Point

Be Gracious

Don't Interrupt

Be Ladylike/Gentlemanly

Open Doors & Pull Out Chairs

Customers Have the Right of Way

Address Customers with Proper Names

Treat Others As You Want To Be Treated

Remember, Customers Are Your **#1** Priority

Manners and etiquette show the gratefulness of a business, its staff and its owner. Look at upscale businesses and their customer service personnel as an example. Think **Rodeo Drive** or upscale hotels, any **cream of the crop** business. One of the most visible characteristics that sets them apart from other like businesses is the obvious polish of their staff and their detailed attention to manners.

♦ They greet you at the door.

♦ They offer you a helping hand.

♦ They cater to the ladies with chivalrous reverence.

- They allow customers to speak freely and openly.
- They escort customers rather than pointing in a general direction.
- They put customers first in every situation.
- They surpass the customer's needs.
- They are polite and formal and conduct themselves in a sophisticated and professional demeanor.

These types of businesses are the epitome of manners.

Goal of Manners:
Convey Gratitude & Respect

Kings and queens are addressed as "Your Majesty." In the military, "Sir" is a title that is learned quickly as a sign of respect and admiration. Can you imagine a private calling his commanding officer "John?" Likewise, address customers formally through the use of proper names (Mr. Jackson, Miss Jones). In situations where you are unaware of the person's name, use "sir" or "ma'am."

Properly addressing customers shows **utmost respect**. Avoid using first names. It can actually be disrespectful and inappropriate unless directed otherwise.

THE GOOD

On a recent morning I drove my car through my usual coffee spot to make my daily purchase. In the course of my minute-long interaction, the cashier thanked me for stopping, thanked me for my order and thanked me again when I paid. She was respectful and shared manners throughout this brief transaction. She was appreciative that I was there and even remembered that I frequent the establishment. Why did I remember it? Because it is so rare to see and hear customer service professionals respond with great manners.

THE BAD

I was looking to buy a new car. At the dealership someone greeted me and told me that they would be with me in a moment. As I made my way around the showroom I was abruptly cut off as another salesman walked directly in front of me. He didn't slow, stop, look at me, say "excuse me," or even realize that he had done so. He forgot about manners and was oblivious to the fact that I was there! I felt like I I was invisible and in the way.

THE UGLY

I approached a checkout counter and set my items down. The cashier grabbed each item, scanned them, then stated, "Twenty-seven thirty-nine." No "Hi!" No smile. No "How are you today, sir?" No "Thank you!" No "Please stop back and see us again." No manners. She literally only muttered some almost unintelligible numbers to me and nothing more!

Sad, but, all too often TRUE

It has become the **NORM** to give our money to companies that allow employees to act without manners and to treat us as if we were nothing more than a wallet.

Your Manners

Examine your customer service manners.

- Are you courteous and polite?
- What about your staff?
- Do they use proper manners?
- Do they use **The BIG 4**?

EXERCISE

Think of real life examples that have happened and discuss them with your customer service staff. Ideally, use situations that have (or could potentially) happen in your business.

Select one Good, one Bad and one Ugly. Make sure that you select examples that focus on areas you believe your staff excels in (the Good) and areas that they need to improve (the Bad & the Ugly).

Role Play with *"The Bad"* and *"The Ugly"* examples. Teach your customer service staff to correctly handle situations with manners and respect.

One Simple Phrase Can Make or Break a Business:

I'm Sorry

Apologies Are FREE!

NOW SERVING 5

Customer service is judged by how problems are addressed and resolved. It is astonishing how many businesses fail this simple customer service test of **excellence**.

Everything that happens to a customer is a business' responsibility, even if it's bad. We are all human and we all make mistakes. Mistakes *will* happen. They happen everywhere. While we can't always avoid mistakes, we can take advantage of the situation and create new loyal customers from these problems and challenges.

Effective Apologies Must Be Handled Promptly

Customers Want To Be Happy

When mistakes occur apologies are **crucial** to preserving customer relationships. A successful apology produces **loyalty** simply because the situation was resolved with complete satisfaction and the customers felt the business had genuine concern for their happiness.

Customers say there is a problem because they want to give you the opportunity to correct the situation and to make them happy. If they didn't care about being happy they wouldn't tell you, and they wouldn't come back.

Be THANKFUL that Customers Complain

Take **advantage** of complaints and view them as opportunities to earn the customer's continued business. You should approach a problem not only as an opportunity to apologize and correct it so that the customer leaves happy, but also as a challenge to turn the customer into a content smiling customer that will return again and again.

Complaints Are Opportunities

The following four step process is simple and will work with any problem situation that might arise. Adhere to these steps to ensure a successful apology and a happy and satisfied customer:

1 ▶ APOLOGIZE
2 ▶ LISTEN
3 ▶ CORRECT
4 ▶ FOLLOW THROUGH

STEP 1

APOLOGIZE

• **Apologize Immediately to the Customer** •

Say "*I'm sorry.*" **Say it immediately** and before you say anything else. An apology is the act of speaking the actual phrase "I'm sorry."

Say It Because You Mean It NOT Because You Have To

In some situations it is acceptable for apologies to be in the form of a written letter or email, but whenever possible a face-to-face encounter is ideal.

While you are addressing a customer that expresses any sort of dissatisfaction with your product or service, the immediate response should be "I'm sorry." Apologies are not what you do (i.e. giving a discount or offering something for free). Apologies are not blaming the situation on company pol-

icy or employees. An apology is more than simply acknowledging the error, misstep or problem; it is a genuine, verbal expression of regret for having failed the customer's expectations. Apologies must be presented professionally and with confidence so that the customer knows that their concerns are taken seriously.

Own It

You are the representative of your business. Whether or not you agree with the customer's complaint or issue is not the initial concern. Your apology isn't necessarily an admission of guilt or wrongdoing in the situation. Rather, your apology is an **empathetic response** and a display of concern that the customer is not happy or satisfied.

A sincere, heartfelt apology not only conveys interest in the customer's satisfaction, but also saves and builds **lifelong** customer relationships and friends. Make it a priority to verify that the situation is resolved to the complete satisfaction of your customer.

Apologies Should Be

- Swift
- Automatic
- Sincere
- Positive

Customers See Through Half-Hearted Apologies

Disgruntled customers will not come back and they will quickly spread the word about their less-than-satisfactory experience. Managers and customer service personnel must be confident and comfortable when conveying apologies. They should not sound rehearsed or repetitious. Nor should the apology make the customer feel as if you are giving in simply for the sake of apologizing. It should always be an honest acknowledgement of the customer's dissatisfaction.

NOT Apologizing Is **NOT** Acceptable

Apologies are mandatory, expected and vital to outstanding customer service. Failure to apologize angers people and pushes them away from your business and toward your competitors. A missing or lackluster apology says that you could care less about your customer's experience and happiness.

Always Apologize!

What an Apology Is NOT

- Ignoring the Problem
- A Nuisance

- Blaming Others
- Going Through the Motions

- Giving In
- Citing "Company Policy"

- Delayed or Untimely
- Becoming Defensive

- Passing the Buck
- What You Do (Giving Something for Free)

STEP 2

LISTEN

• Listen With Concern •

After you have taken the time to offer a formal apology you should let the customer explain their concerns and situation. Make sure that you will not be interrupted by others and by all means **do not interrupt** the customer.

■■■■■■■■■■■■■■■■■■■■■■■■■■■■

Let Customers Complete their Explanation Before Speaking

■■■■■■■■■■■■■■■■■■■■■■■■■■■■

It becomes cumbersome and frustrating for a customer to continually repeat the specifics of their situation, especially to multiple people. You may even want to take notes about the circumstances.

By allowing the customer to explain the situation without disruption you will accomplish a couple of things. **First**, the customer will have the opportunity to tell you what happened from their point of view. Many times customers want nothing more than an apology and someone to listen to them.

Customers Don't Always Want Something For FREE

Second, it gives the customers time to settle down and relax. **Plus**, they'll know that you're taking the situation seriously because you're giving them your time and respect. **Finally**, it allows you the opportunity to completely assess the situation from the customer's point of view. You can also then gauge their level of dissatisfaction to make an informed determination of what steps you have to take to correct the problem.

1. React Immediately
2. Make Eye Contact
3. Speak Clearly
4. Give the Customer Your Undivided Attention
5. Don't Interrupt or Argue
6. Remain Positive & Professional
7. Be Truthful & Honest
8. Focus on What the Customer Is Saying
9. Take Notes About the Problem
10. Watch Your Body Language
    – Don't cross your arms
11. Follow Through
12. Follow Up

Never Argue

It serves no purpose to argue or disagree with a customer. It will only further exacerbate the problem and make it even more difficult for you to recover from the challenge that you are addressing.

The Customer's Perception of the Circumstances Is Always Accurate

Your perception may be different and contradictory. You have to look at the situation from the customer's point of view. Simply acknowledge their point of view, apologize and correct the problem to make them happy. You don't have to agree with the perception but you do have to acknowledge it.

Here's a great example - I ordered chicken strips at a restaurant. I was served fish instead. I pointed this out to the server. The server insisted that it was chicken without even looking at the plate. She then went to ask the kitchen who, she said, agreed with her. "It was chicken." They made a big ordeal out of it, argued with me, "I'm sure, it's chicken." She even got other people involved and made me wait while they discussed whether it swam or clucked.

It would have been so much easier, faster and satisfactory to me if the server simply said, "I'm sorry, let me fix that for you!" Instead, her implication was, "This dumb guy actually thinks that I served him fish instead of chicken. (*It really was fish!*) He thinks that I don't know the difference" She didn't care whether I was happy or not. She was insistent on being right.

STEP 3

CORRECT

• **Correct the Problem** •

Take the necessary steps to correct the problem at hand. Issue a refund, replace an unacceptable item, offer an alternative product or service, or whatever is appropriate for your particular business.

Some businesses empower their customer service personnel to correct problems and address issues. On the surface this is a great concept because the customer's needs are ideologically being met quickly. However, you cannot be certain that the problem situations are being handled to your satisfaction, let alone to your customer's. **Role playing** can help with your evaluation of resolving issues by empowering employees.

NOTHING Matches the Power of Management Involvement when Problems Arise

STEP 4

FOLLOW THROUGH

• **Ensure Complete Satisfaction** •

If, by this point, management has not been involved in the situation it is essential that they become involved now. A manager is a recognized representative of the business and makes the apology official.

In the Customer's Eyes Management *Is* the Business

Management is trained to handle these situations with confidence and should be the final verification that the customer is indeed satisfied with the way that the entire experience was handled.

The size or significance of the customer's concern should not designate the manager's involvement. If your customers convey that they are not pleased with your service or product **in any way** management must commit to resolving the situation and becoming personally involved. Only when management is truly concerned, can they be certain that their customers are happy and plan to return. Management involvement should be personal and prompt. It can generally be a quick conversation that will reinforce and ensure that the customer's situation has been corrected. Follow-through may also be via telephone or letter, but it should never be delayed.

EXCELLENT Customer Service Demands that a Manager Follow Up

Don't abandon, ignore or delegate this responsibility to another person or employee.

Management Must Take Responsibility for the Problem

Problems should be dealt with head on and effectively. Management should ensure that the outcome is complete customer satisfaction.

Most importantly, remember that your apology and how you apologize can turn a problem situation into a **positive** and **caring** customer service experience. Show them that you are a class act and are serious about satisfaction. Effective apologies impress customers and turn them into repeat customers. Situations like this will leave the customer smiling and impressed with the experience, as well as you and your company.

• • • Apology Accepted • • •

A flight was delayed due to mechanical problems. The gate attendant promptly **apologized** for the delay and informed the waiting passengers of the details. Passengers were directed to the service counter where attendants empathetically **listened** to passenger questions and concerns about their travels.

For many, the situation was **corrected** with a simple explanation or assignment to an alternate flight. Once on board, the airline **followed through** and distributed discount vouchers that could be used for future flights, cocktails or frequent flyer miles.

On top of that, the airline's Customer Care Manager sent a personal letter to passengers, explaining that "loyal customers are the key to any company's success." The **follow up** letter also announced that the airline was depositing additional frequent flyer miles into passenger accounts.

WOW! *Now that's impressive!*

ROLE PLAY

Pose a situation (or use the ones listed below) to your customer service staff and have them handle the apology using the 4-step process:

1 ▶ **APOLOGIZE**
2 ▶ **LISTEN**
3 ▶ **CORRECT**
4 ▶ **FOLLOW THROUGH**

Role Play with the following example situations:

A

Dental patient, Betty Molar had an appointment at 10:00am. It is now 10:30am and she is *still* sitting in the waiting room, looking rather agitated and thumping her foot.

B

Mr. Rider calls ABC Insurance because money for his policy has been withdrawn from his checking account twice.

C

Autumn mistakenly asked for blonde hair dye. After the stylist completed the job she turned the chair around to face the mirror. Autumn became upset, "I asked for black dye, not blonde."

Exceed Expectations

If you truly want to make a lasting impression, learn to go above and beyond. **Do something unexpected** – follow up an apology with a hand written letter, an e-mail or a telephone call. This will strengthen your **dedication to superior customer service**. It will be a pleasant surprise, will "wow" your customers and it will show them that you are sincerely concerned about their happiness and complete satisfaction. These actions are the standards and the basis of great, lifelong, business relationships.

People Talk Because they Want Someone to

Listen

www.customerserviceisfree.com

Listening Is FREE!

Listening to customer feedback about your business, your product and customer service is one of the most **vital** things that you can devote time to. When you listen, your customers will tell you if they approve of what you are doing and if they feel that you have room for improvement.

Be thankful that customers are taking the time to share their comments whether they're compliments or complaints. In fact, be more thankful to field complaints that provide the opportunity to correct the situations and improve customer service.

■■■■■■■■■■■■■■■■■■■■■■■■■■■■■■

The **BEST** Suggestions Come from Customers

■■■■■■■■■■■■■■■■■■■■■■■■■■■■■■

Your customers want you to listen because they want you to **succeed**. Otherwise, they would simply take their business elsewhere. It's up to you to pay attention, listen and take action.

Listening Is NOT Hearing

Listening is the art of learning and choosing to extract pertinent information from conversations and situations. Great listeners get to the heart of the matter and react with perceptiveness, reason and a sense of urgency. It requires tuning into the facts, the tone and the relevance. Most importantly a great listener acts on what he discovers in the process.

Your customers will present you with opportunities to listen in a vast array of ways:

- Conversation
- Letters
- E-Mails
- Comment Cards
- Questionnaires
- Online Surveys

You can seek out customer reviews that are widely read on internet forums. You might even hear second-hand comments about your business from colleagues or family members.

What Are you Listening for?

As discussed previously, you are listening for the customer's recounting of the situation, the facts, how it happened (or didn't) from their point of view. This is what the customer is unhappy about and wants you to address. Pay close attention to the details. Be respectful and allow the customer to speak **uninterrupted** and with your undivided attention. Take notes if necessary and always repeat the facts back for confirmation. A great listener is **empathetic, understanding and apologetic**, never argumentative or willing to offer up excuses.

Listen For The Problem

Was there a particular flaw or person responsible for the customer's letdown? **Where did things go wrong?** A great listener also notices what is *not* said? Are important details left out? Look at the BIG picture. Is this a problem that other customers are encountering as well, a recurring situation that has just been brought to your attention? Address the situation to guarantee that other customers don't have to experience the same situation.

- There's water on the floor
- The price is marked wrong
- The temperature is cold
- The sales lady was rude

Use specific examples for training and development. In other words, what can your customer service staff learn from the customer's experience?

Listen for the Resolution

What can you do to correct a situation and ensure that the customer is happy and convinced that you are genuine about their concerns? Occasionally a customer will tell you what they want; replace the item, refund their money, etc. More often than not you will be left to make a decision based on how well you listened to the details. Whatever you do, **do something for the customer.**

Listen with Your Actions

Your reaction to the situation shows the customer that you are compassionate about their experience and that you are serious about customer service. If you listen to a customer or read a letter from them but do nothing, it's **meaningless**. You are passing up a golden opportunity. Show them that you are sincerely thankful for their time and their opinion. It will come back to you ten fold!

Be Prepared to Act on Comments

Soliciting customer feedback can open your eyes to hidden issues and problems. You can't listen to customer comments if you are stuck in the back office. Wander the sales floor, showroom, restaurant or business and encourage comments that create opportunities to listen and improve. Comments can be taken from direct conversation and interaction with customers by simply asking. Inquire about the product or the service. e.g. Did you enjoy your stay with us last night?

Collecting information by means of comment cards, questionnaires or surveys can become overwhelming because of the sheer volume of information. Be certain that you are as prepared to listen to each of those solicited replies as you would a hand written letter.

If you are conducting an online survey and ask an open ended question to which a customer replies unfavorably, make sure that you have a system in place to address that individual. Their comments are just as valuable.

Your Business Depends on It

If you have no intention of addressing issues you will do much more **harm** than good. No action or response is the equivalent of ignoring a potential customer wandering, helplessly, through a furniture showroom. Hopefully, the goal of solicited responses is to improve your customer service. React to each and every response with urgency and extreme importance.

Don't Ask if You Don't Want to Know

FOCUS GROUPS

If you **really** want to know what your customers say about you, hold focus group meetings. These open forums are very effective for gathering useful comments, constructive criticism and suggestions from your customers' point of view. The most productive participants are regular and first time customers.

Regular Customers	First Time Customers
Provide an honest evaluation and truthful constructive criticism	Provide unbiased insight into first impressions

People will be *thrilled* that you want to listen to what their thoughts and ideas are about your business. That's the whole purpose of a focus group, to gather vital information. It's important to conduct study groups in a formal and structured manner so that you are able to achieve your goal of **listening**.

■■■■■■■■■■■■■■■■■■■■■■■■■■■■
Set Specific Goals and Keep on Track
■■■■■■■■■■■■■■■■■■■■■■■■■■■■

Ask and listen for areas of customer service that you can improve.

Pointed Questions

- What do you like the most about our service?

- What would you do to improve our quality of service?

- What do you like least about our service?

- How would you rate our customer service in relation to our competition?

- Why would you choose to go to the competition instead of our business?

- What do you tell your family and friends about us?

Listen carefully and take notes about these issues and solutions. I can't think of a better way to listen to what your customers have to say about your service than this open, honest conversation.

Your customers will feel honored to be a part of your endeavors to improve customer service for their future visits with you. **Thank** your customers graciously for the opportunity to listen to their thoughts and recommendations.

To be truly concerned about superior customer service understand that you cannot accept **mediocrity**. Strive for stellar comments and accept nothing less. In your listening endeavors, search out the mediocre statements. Don't settle for less than great customer service experiences for your customers.

"The room service was *ok*."

"The girl who helped us did what she was *supposed* to."

"Everything was *alright*."

These comments are clues that the service could have been better. When these comments are shared you must request more information from the customer. For business' sake you need to find out why their experiences were "just okay" instead of "spectacular," "fantastic" or "the best ever."

Information Comes from Every Direction

You must actively and consciously listen. You may overhear a customer's comment that is detrimental to your business but was not directed to you. **Address it.** It might be your only opportunity to salvage the relationship with the customer. Apologize that you overheard but address what you listened to.

Address issues and problems that you hear from a second hand source. Go to every length to contact that person. Imagine how impressed they will be when they find out that you actually listened to what their acquaintance told you and followed through with it. They will certainly get the message that you care about their satisfaction.

Satisfied Customers Become Regular Clientele

Listen to your regular customers. They are one of your most **valuable** sources of information. They will be forthright and candid because they know what to expect from your business. More than anyone, they want to continue enjoying the highest level of customer service that they have come to expect from you. They will know if something is amiss even if you don't.

■ ■ ■ ■ ■ ■ ■ ■ ■ ■
Take it to Heart
■ ■ ■ ■ ■ ■ ■ ■ ■ ■

Non-verbal listening is key as well. Observing facial expressions, stances, eye-rolls and other customer actions can be very revealing. A sour look on someone's face demands further investigation. A confused customer looking around requires immediate attention. Crossed arms relay unease and dissatisfaction that will quickly need to be addressed. People constantly speak with their actions but we don't always listen.

Observation Is Silent Listening

Although you surely have a hectic schedule, I **highly** recommend that you allow time in your routine that's dedicated to listening to and addressing customer input. Don't forget to listen to your employees as well. They are a wealth of knowledge and if you don't listen to them, someone else will.

10 Traits of a GREAT Listener

1 • Attentive
2 • Empathetic
3 • Responsive
4 • Professional
5 • Appreciative
6 • Observant
7 • Patient
8 • Respectful
9 • Resolute
10 • Accessible

EXERCISE

Are you listening on the internet?

Search for your business on the internet and look for

Reviews • Posts • Forums

Use these written listening opportunities to identify problems and help train your managers and customer service staff.

Mechanics of Listening

1- Make Direct **Eye Contact**

2- Remain **Focused**, Don't Stray

3- Lean Forward in **Interest**, Lend an Ear

4- **Speak Clearly** and Professionally

5- Take **Notes**

6- Nod Your Head in **Understanding**

7- **Verbalize** Agreement, "I Understand"

8- **Repeat** the Facts Back for Clarity

LISTENING PLAN

The following form is a great exercise to get you **focused** on listening. It's a tool that you can use individually or with a management team or even with co-workers. Document as much information as you can and include any accompanying paperwork with the form for future reference. I would recommend using these forms in an ongoing fashion whether it be monthly, quarterly, etc. It will keep you on your toes and help you to constantly remain focused on improving customer service.

LISTENING PLAN

DIRECTIONS - Using this template, develop a working plan to identify areas of customer service that can be improved upon by means of a listening action, such as a customer survey, informal questioning or comment cards. Once the plan is developed be sure to adhere to the plan and hold responsible persons accountable. Review your progress with all involved parties on a routine basis.
Upon completion, review the results and gauge your success. Determine if this is a plan worth repeating, note pros and cons and make recommendations for future similar Customer Service Listening Plans.

PROJECT -

OBJECTIVE -

Action/Task	Person(s) Responsible	Target Date	Completion Date	Comments/Results

Was this Customer Service Listening Plan Successful?   YES   NO

What were the benefits of the results of the plan?

Should the plan be repeated?   YES   NO

IF YES, what recommendations would you make for a similar project?

Customer Service Is FREE © 2010 www.customerserviceisfree.com

Develop a **Listening Plan** to identify areas of customer service that can be improved upon by means of a listening action, such as a customer survey, informal questioning or comment cards.

Find a **FREE** printable version of the Listening Plan on our website, www.customerserviceisfree.com.

Thank **Every** *Customer,* **Every** *Time*

www.customerserviceisfree.com

NOW SERVING 7

Appreciation Is FREE!

The hardware store recently celebrated Customer Appreciation Week. Does that mean that they don't appreciate their customers the rest of the year? Clearly, this is just a marketing strategy to keep customers coming back by handing out trinkets and discounts. Surely, the hardware store does appreciate their customers every day. But what do they do the rest of the year?

How *Does* a Business Show Appreciation?

Appreciation can be shared in a multitude of ways. It's not as simple as just smiling and thanking your customers! There's quite a bit to consider: attitude, demeanor, sincerity and satisfaction, among others. Appreciation requires conscientious **dedication** to customer service.

It Starts with Attitude

A positive attitude is **paramount** to successfully expressing gratitude. In order to share sincere appreciation and heartfelt thanks you must have **passion** and a genuine concern. Your care and conviction must be apparent in your speech as well as your disposition.

Don't go overboard with exaggerated, patronizing thanks. You want to avoid sounding rehearsed or repetitive. Above all, don't let customers feel that you are going through the motions just because you have to. Customers will see right through transparent meaningless statements. Be sincere and customers will take you seriously.

Showing respect for your customers shows that you appreciate them. After all, customers have chosen you over your competition.

Customers *Deserve* Your Respect

Attitudes and respect come across in your tone and actions. They express thanks as well.

- ♦ Speak to customers and treat them with grace, dignity and professional mannerism.
- ♦ Mind what you say and avoid slang terms and conversation.
- ♦ Stand straight, don't slouch, don't fidget.

- Be cautious of interacting too casually and maintain decorum.

- Never, *never* use profanity in your place of employment - no exceptions no matter who you are speaking to.

- Pay attention to your body language as well. Don't look off in the distance, focus on the customer.

- Remain professional at all times.

Voice Your Thanks

True professionals thank *every* customer, *every* time, without fail! You must be **consistent** and **persistent**. There is absolutely no acceptable reason for not saying thank you, no matter the industry, the size of the business or the location.

Lead by example and set the standard for your customer service staff. Hold them accountable. Make it clear to them that you expect customer appreciation to be obvious. Your staff can be thankful and appreciative, but it doesn't mean a thing if they don't share it. Actually, it is quite disrespectful and inconsiderate not to show appreciation. Offering thanks is not only courteous, but it's also professional and expected.

Demonstrating thanks doesn't mean doling out coffee mugs or pens with your logo on them. It doesn't have to cost you anything, and honestly it shouldn't.

Appreciation Is Best Expressed Through Excellent Customer Service

It's Attentive
It's Honest
It's Personal

When you hold your business, your employees and yourself to the **highest standards** you ensure not only satisfaction, but also the truest expression of gratitude. Exceptional customer service is always the most sincere way to show customer appreciation on a daily basis. The experience is appreciation in and of itself.

If There Is Only One Thing that a Business Is Thankful for, it Should be **Customers**

Obviously, without customers there would be no business. Treat every customer as if you were indebted to them for your job, because you are. Customers are fundamentally responsible for main-

Always Remember:

Nothing Is More Important than Offering Thanks!

taining the livelihood of your income and continued employment. You should oblige all customers with thoughtful and honest appreciation.

Sincere expressions of gratitude are the **building blocks** of life long customer relationships and the basis of excellent customer service. The goal should be to make customers feel wanted and welcome.

Everyone Enjoys Feeling Appreciated

If customers don't feel appreciated they will certainly make other choices and take their business elsewhere.

As you can see, being appreciative involves much more than going through the motions. It requires a real sense of **concern** for your customers' happiness and utmost gratitude for their continued patronage.

Remember to be appreciative of your employees, colleagues and coworkers as well. Employees that feel less than appreciated don't always perform with customers' best interests in mind. Happy, appreciated personnel provide smiling and honest customer service. It's service from the heart because they know they are appreciated. The same standards apply when expressing employee appreciation - positive attitude, demeanor, sincerity, respect and satisfaction goes a long way.

Your Employees Are *Your* Customers

Customer Service Is FREE

A little appreciation and a simple "thank you" builds lasting relationships and healthy, **profitable** businesses.

Notes of APPRECIATION

A friend that manages a large department store recently related a perfect example. He had just received a **hand written note** of thanks from his director of operations. He was pleasantly surprised and impressed. He felt valued because his efforts were recognized. He posted the note on a bulletin board where anyone could read it and share in his pride. The value of that note was **priceless**.

Recently, while sorting through the mail, I spotted a small hand addressed envelope that looked as if it were an invitation. I opened it to find a personally written thank you card from the manager of the car repair shop that I visited the week prior. I must say that I was positively surprised that he took the time to express his gratitude for my recent repair. I was impressed so much that I saved the note and have told several friends about it. That's the outcome of his appreciation: continued business from me and **priceless word of mouth advertising** to my friends, all likely to bring him new customers, more business and profit!

EXERCISE

Random Acts of Appreciation

Weekly (or some regular basis), choose a number of customers (5 - 20) to contact by telephone, written letter or email to thank them for their business. This personal touch will show your true dedication to customer service and your sincere appreciation for their continued patronage. Trust me, they will remember the call (or letter) and will share it with their family and friends.

Hopefully your contacts will have had a great experience, but be prepared that some of them may not be glowing reviews. You might have to do some damage control. However, take advantage of the opportunity to correct the situation and address it now.

T ruthful
H eartfelt
A pparent
N ecessary
K ind
S incere

Give Sincere Thanks for Each and EVERY Customer!

Awards are great **FREE** tools to give to employees. Try giving them to **customers** for memorable and priceless appreciation. Customer Appreciation Awards are available online as well.

Find a **FREE** printable version of this Appreciation Award on our website, www.customerserviceisfree.com.

Wow Factor

\ˈwau̇ ˈfak-tər\
noun

a positive, 'talkable' and shareable service moment that leaves a customer in awe of the high level of service and/or the performance of the service professional.

The WOW Factor Is FREE!

NOW SERVING 8

The Wow Factor is service that is so good, so unique, so memorable, so impressionable or so positively unexpected that the customer leaves thinking, "*Wow! The service was awesome!*" or "*Wow! I didn't anticipate that!*" Their customer service experience was heightened by the fact that their expectations were surpassed and they recognized and remembered it.

- That little extra step
- That special service
- That added touch

WOW! That Was Great!

That's the **Wow Factor**. The Wow Factor is not something material that you give to someone. Rather it's something that you do, and quite often it's the little things that you do that make the biggest impact. It's great service.

FREE Is Something Every Business Can Afford

Every business can create memorable experiences. This doesn't apply just to businesses that are flush with cash or high-end, exclusive businesses. The amount of money a customer spends should not determine the quality of service that is expected. Quite the contrary, the quality of service will make your customers want to spend more at your business.

Wow Your Customers, the Business Will Follow

Think about a great service experience that you felt you *needed* to relate to other people. What was it about that experience that made you want to share it? What made you want to write a complimentary letter or tell the manager about that great experience? Whatever it is that you remember and want to share is the Wow Factor. It's something that was unexpected and made you want to talk to your family and friends about it.

It's Talkable

The Wow Factor is a service step that stops you in your tracks and makes you pause, reflect and feel stunned and impressed all at the same time. It's those things that go above and beyond, the extraordinary and the unforgettable. They set you apart from the competition and from mediocre service.

★ An employee walks you to your car with an umbrella when it's raining

★ You receive a follow up phone call to ensure that you were satisfied

★ You discover that the return policy really was *no questions asked*

★ A sales clerk greets you by name

The Wow Factor Promotes
PRICELESS
Word of Mouth Advertising

How do you train the Wow Factor? Use example situations. They are the best way to relate the Wow Factor concept. Take advantage of opportunities that you see in your day to day operations. Call the examples out and recognize the employees that take pleasure in **wowing** your customers so that the rest of your personnel know what the Wow Factor is and understand it!

Train the Wow Factor

1 ♦ Wow Factor Award - Give awards or other public acknowledgement.

2 ♦ Post It - Share positive letters and emails from wowed customers.

3 ♦ Call Out - Mention Wow Factor situations in meetings and newsletters and discuss them.

4 ♦ Talk About It - Talk about The Wow Factor at *every* opportunity in casual conversation with staff.

5 ♦ Brainstorm - Have open discussions with customer service staff and management about The Wow Factor.

6 ♦ Role Play - Act out situations in groups, create examples.

7 ♦ Personalize It - Send a personal, hand-written note to an employee's home in recognition of wowing a customer. They *will* talk about it to everyone.

8 ♦ Teach - Train staff to do one thing that makes a Wow impact with every customer.

9 ♦ Life Experiences - What Examples can you share from your interactions as a customer? Where were you wowed? What wows you?

10 ♦ Lead By Example - Set the standard so employees know what's expected of them.

Talk about it **constantly** so your employees know that it's expected and a part of your customer service **culture** and **standards**. Train your staff that going above and beyond is always expected and never an exception.

The Wow Factor is going that extra mile and exceeding expectations. But the greatest value of the Wow Factor is that it forces you to always improve your quality and level of service. The Wow Factor causes you to routinely re-evaluate your service standards and to look for ways to raise that bar.

Sadly, the bar is so low in regards to customer service today, that customers have come to accept substandard and even poor service.

Management **Cannot** Accept Mediocrity

Management must lead by example and strive to raise customers' expectations. The Wow Factor starts at the top. It starts with you! If your service standards are not getting better, they are getting worse because someone else's are always getting better.

You Must be the One that Is Getting Better in Order to Excel

The Wow Factor will set you apart from your competition. It will make you stand out. It will make your customers talk about your business and service.

Things that Make You Go **WOW!**

1 Everyone knows, Disney World does everything **BIG** and with a smile because it is, after all, the *Happiest Place on Earth*! I recently visited the park on my birthday. They wowed me with one of the simplest service steps that I have ever experienced that cost them next to nothing: they gave me a birthday button with my name on it to wear for the day. I thought it was a bit corny. But, let me tell you that every employee (yes, every one) that I encountered, and even park guests, wished me a Happy Birthday by name because of the button! I was **WOWED**! I'm sure they trained their "cast members" to wish a Happy Birthday to everyone that wears a birthday button. It's ingenious really. I've told everyone about it and it's in every picture of me from that day! What better advertising could they ask for?

2 I sent a package using overnight service from a small, locally owned wrap and ship center. The service was polite and efficient but nothing really memorable. What Wowed me actually happened the following day. I received a phone call from the business. I immediately thought that something happened to my package. I was wrong. The girl on the phone was making a courtesy call to tell me that the package had indeed been delivered on time! I was **WOWED**! It was completely unexpected and truly memorable. I've told everyone about it and I will never go anywhere else to mail a package!

I went to the grocery store to pick up a few items. I didn't think that I needed a basket. Suddenly my arms were overflowing with items that I hadn't planned on buying. Out of nowhere an employee appeared to offer me a shopping basket. I was thankful and impressed that they were even aware of my situation. I was **WOWED**!

As you can see from these examples, the Wow Factor is often simple and quick. They are thoughtful, helpful and memorable. The impact that *Wows* have on customer service experiences is impressive and invaluable. These experiences start the **Circle of Wow**. You create an exceptional experience enhanced by the Wow Factor. The Wowed customers come back because the service was memorable which gives you a new chance to Wow them!

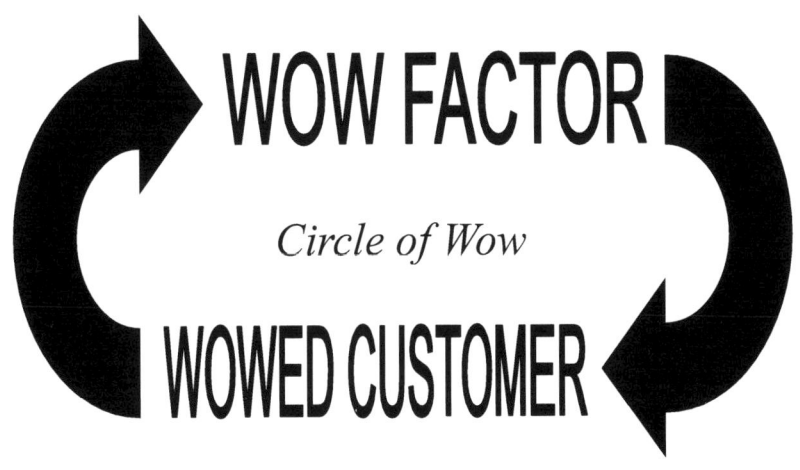

Circle of Wow

EXERCISE

Something to Talk About

TOP 10

Schedule a brainstorming session with the your management team and the customer service staff.

Discuss specific ways that your business can **WOW** your customers. Write them down and make a **Top 10 List**.

Post this list in a location that is very visible to the entire customer service staff.

Update this list regularly as customer expectations are raised.

Presenting awards in recognition of Wow Factor situations is a great training tool. Employees love to be recognized for their achievements.

Find a **FREE** printable version of the WOW Award on our website, www.customerserviceisfree.com.

What Spreads Faster than a Brush Fire on a Windy Day?

An
Attitude

Attitudes Are FREE!

What type of attitude are you choosing to portray and emulate to both staff and customers alike?

The only acceptable answer is a **positive** attitude. Positive attitudes are very apparent to people you interact with and they create a welcoming and comfortable environment. They convey happiness, sincerity, dedication and passion. Most importantly, when you have a positive, healthy attitude those around you will share in your attitude.

Positive Attitudes Are Contagious

In other words, you will have a subconscious effect on others' mental outlook. Your upbeat demeanor will unquestionably persuade people to also be positive. People will want to share in your positivity, will want to work with you, will want to work *for* you, will want to listen to you and help you out.

They Will Want to be Positive, Like You

The **synergy** that positive attitudes create is unmatched! They are incredibly powerful and influential. Positive attitudes can move mountains.

Your attitude is one of few things that you have **complete control** over. Your boss can't control it. Your spouse can't control it. The weather can't control it. Even the economy can't control it.

Only You Can Decide to Have a Positive Attitude

Your **attitude determines your course**, how your day goes, how you interact with people and how people will interact with you. A great attitude is the difference between a mediocre customer interaction and a superior customer service experience that will be remembered.

If you "wake up on the wrong side of the bed" and

decide that you are going to be miserable, you are setting yourself up for a terrible day! The people that you interact with are going to be hesitant to approach you. You are going to attract nothing but negative energy. Bad attitudes are contagious, just like positive attitudes. So, when you give attitude, give positive attitude! It *will* rub off on others.

Positive Attitudes Are Vital to Excellent Customer Service

Your front lines must be cheerful and optimistic, even exuberant. Employee interactions with customers should *always* be positive. It is *never* acceptable to complain to a customer and there is no excuse for not being pleasant and courteous. Hold your staff accountable and be certain that they know that only positive attitudes will be acceptable.

What attitude are your customer service employees sharing with your customers? Do you know?

A friend of mine went to a business and encountered a rude employee. Later she told me, "They were so nasty and mean. I don't deserve to be treated like that. I'll never go back!" Believe me, when she said *never,* she meant it. Her decision was based on one employee that didn't have a positive attitude.
One employee. One time. One transaction.
That's all it took to lose a customer.

Make it a priority to know your employee's attitudes!

 **One person** with a bad attitude can do a lot of damage. Being negative is an invitation for others to also be negative.

Your customer service staff are your ambassadors and they represent you to the public. They must possess positive attitudes. No one wants to deal with an "attitude," especially customers, and no one has to.

Positively Positive

I worked with a girl that had to be the happiest person that I ever met. She was always **smiling**, always **laughing**, **never complained** and really just had a **cheerful** and **uplifting** demeanor. She was a pleasure to talk to and to work with. I looked forward to seeing her every day because you couldn't help but feel positive when she was near. She made people want to help her and be like her because she was always so willing to offer a smile and assistance. She was the epitome of positive attitude!

Managers attitudes are contagious and spread like the plague. They must be held accountable for their own attitudes by setting the example. They must maintain a positive attitude and be constantly aware of their actions.

 *"Do as I say, not as I do"*
Won't Cut It

Negative thoughts and attitudes must be checked at the door and the focus should be on the customer. It is imperative to psych yourself up and have a positive mental outlook.

Positive Dispositions Make All the Difference

If you truly care enough about customer service and satisfaction, your efforts and results will be apparent and appreciated. One person with a great attitude is all it takes. A successful, positive experience begins with one positive attitude at the top that trickles down to all of the employees. People with positive attitudes accept nothing less. They make work fun, energetic and exciting. Plus, they never let anything get the best of them. They create an environment that is welcoming and productive.

Only Positive Attitudes Are Acceptable

An employee once told me that they were rude to a customer because the customer had a bad attitude! **Really!** I was shocked. I had to explain to the employee that they had a definitive **obligation** as a representative of the company to always be friendly, courteous and positive no matter what the circumstances. When dealing with a customer that is a challenge, I recommend focusing on the positive to make a lasting impression and a superior experience that the customer will be pleased with.

A great employee realizes that a positive attitude is **essential** for an overall positive customer service experience. If you approach any circumstance with a negative frame of mind, then your results will be negative as well. Likewise, if you approach situations with a positive attitude, you will get **positive results**.

Don't Let Problems Get You Down

Keep in mind that problems are nothing more than opportunities to maintain your positive attitude and a challenge to satisfy customers. Your position must convey your eagerness to please.

OPPORTUNITIES

Tackle all problem situations as opportunities and turn them into positive experiences that you can learn from. After all, you can't change the past but you can put a positive spin on it!

Positive Attitudes
=
Positive Customer Experiences

Positive Bottom Lines

www.customerserviceisfree.com

Check Your Attitude
A Self Examination

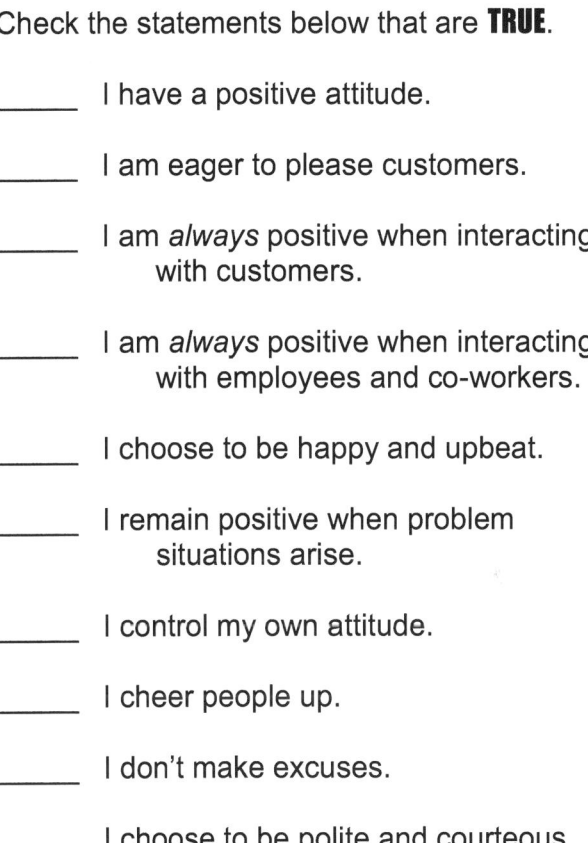

Check the statements below that are **TRUE**.

_____ I have a positive attitude.

_____ I am eager to please customers.

_____ I am *always* positive when interacting with customers.

_____ I am *always* positive when interacting with employees and co-workers.

_____ I choose to be happy and upbeat.

_____ I remain positive when problem situations arise.

_____ I control my own attitude.

_____ I cheer people up.

_____ I don't make excuses.

_____ I choose to be polite and courteous.

How many were true for you? If you left even one unchecked (false), then you have room for improvement.

Choose to Have a Positive Attitude, You'll Be Happy You Did!

Find a printable version of this Self Examination on our website, www.customerserviceisfree.com.

Present awards to employees that foster great attitudes in the workplace. Their positive impact on customer service deserves recognition.

Find a **FREE** printable version of the Positivity Award on our website, www.customerserviceisfree.com.

Follow Through
to Ensure Satisfaction

www.customerserviceisfree.com

Follow Through Is FREE!

A personal banker told me that she was going to review my checking account to find a way to save me money in fees. She said she would get back with me. That was four months ago!

Don't Drop the Ball

In customer service this is a prime example of dropping the ball. The banker had great intentions. She was **proactive** and sought me out. She went the extra mile and **wowed** me. But she didn't make it the whole mile. She left me stranded somewhere along the way, wondering why she didn't get back with me. It certainly makes me think twice about banking with her in the future.

If she had followed through with her promise, I would have been ecstatic! I would have told others that she helped save me money.

Failure to **Follow Through** Destroys Customers Faith & Damages Relationships

Follow Through Is an Unwritten Promise

You promise to satisfy customers. If you do not ensure customer satisfaction you have broken your promise. Some people may find that hard to forgive.

KEEP PROMISES YOUR

- ◆ If you tell someone that you will get back with them, **do it**.
- ◆ If you offer to return a phone call, **do so**.
- ◆ If you ask for constructive criticism in the form of a survey, **respond to it**.
- ◆ If you receive feedback by means of a comment card, letter or e-mail, **reply**.
- ◆ If you offer to get a manager involved, **verify** the manager's involvement.

Follow Through Requires Involvement, Care, Concern and Honesty

Successful follow through means that the customer is happy, needs no further assistance and that the transaction is completed to the customer's satisfaction. The customer should have no unanswered questions and should never be left hanging. I *still* have many questions for the banker. A simple phone call would have been great.

You can have the **best intentions**, the right tools at your fingertips and even the best training programs, but, they are worthless if there is no accountability for follow through. Follow through and its implementation is only attained through training, dedication and awareness.

Follow through involves taking steps to ensure that expectations are met and quality and consistency are maintained. Be **proactive** and seek out problem situations *before* they become customer complaints. Failure to follow through, by any employee at any level, shows a complete disregard for customer satisfaction and is the result of poor, ineffective management.

Follow Through

- **Immediate and Urgent**
- **Take Charge of Difficult Situations**
- **Ensure Satisfaction**
- **Proactive**
- **Keep Customers Informed**
- **Fulfill Your Promises**
- **Have Pride and Confidence**
- **Address Mediocrity**
- **Passion**
- **Commitment**

Sense of Urgency Is Essential

Effective follow through must be timely as well. Follow through loses its efficacy the longer the customer has to wait for it. If a customer is looking for a particular piece of clothing in your store, they want the item **NOW**. They certainly don't want to wait for you to finish a conversation with another employee or to put other inventory away. The customer honestly doesn't care if it is your department or not.

Follow Through Until the Customer's Needs Are Met

If you are unable to answer an inquiry satisfactorily or are not trained to provide what the customer needs, seek out the appropriate person that can offer the proper assistance.

Follow through with the customer and the person that you sought out to be **certain** that the customer's needs are met. Never tell someone you can't help them or that it is not your responsibility. You are the expert on your product and you are there solely to provide the customer with great service and expert information. An appropriate response would be "I will be happy to find out for you." A little extra effort is often required to follow through and ensure great customer service.

"I Don't Know" Should Never Be Spoken

Your efforts should focus on training your staff to follow through and to know when management involvement is required. Employees that do not follow through because of a lack of concern or an unwillingness to respond to situations can be very **costly** to your business.

Teach staff that if they sense any degree of dissatisfaction, management needs to be alerted. Train staff to know that if you have to **apologize**, even for something minor, management should be actively involved with the customer's experience to completion.

When Do You Follow Through?

Furthermore, your customer service staff should never have to ask,

"Would you like me to get my manager?"

If they are even **thinking** about asking that question, that means that a manager needs to be a party to the conversation and resolution.

CAUTION: FOLLOW THROUGH REQUIRED

▶ **Customers Looking Around , Seeking Assistance**

▶ **Customers Asking Questions About Policy**

▶ **Customer Appears Agitated, Perplexed or Angry**

▶ **Customer Responds "OK" or "Alright" When Asked "How was…?"**

Management involvement and extra effort is always required when problems arise. Keep customers informed and updated. Communicate with them every step of the way and follow through with them until the situation is satisfactorily resolved.

FOLLOW UP

Effective follow through also requires follow up. Follow up includes **interaction** after the fact with the customer to extend an apology as well as a thank you for allowing you to correct the situation. It's necessary to **discuss** the situation with customer service employees to ensure that the same issues do not arise again. Follow up means taking the necessary steps to minimize the occurrence of a similar problem.

- Ignoring the Situation
- Citing Company Policy
- "That's not my job."
- "I think so?" ~ Guessing
- "I don't know" ~ Ignorance
- Going Through the Motions
- Turning Responsibility Over to Someone Else
- Being Half-Hearted About the Follow Through
- Not Caring
- Out of Sight Out of Mind

FAIL

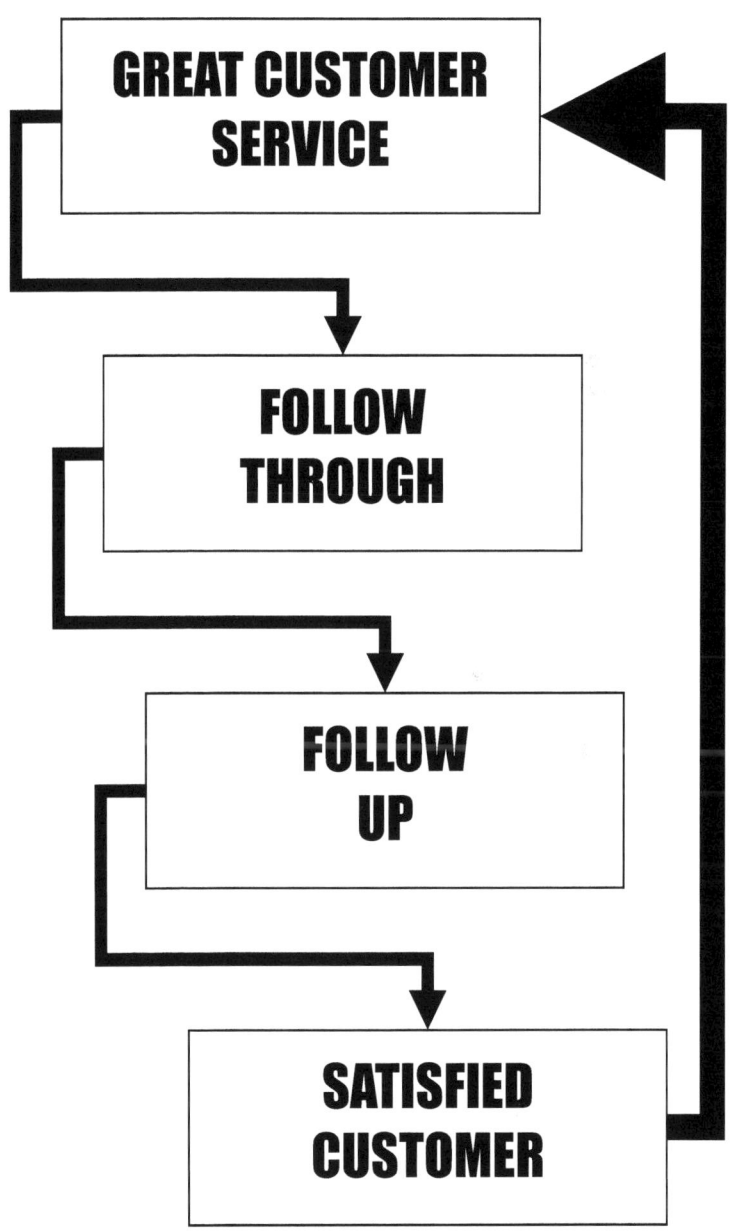

Tools of Follow Through

Checklists - Carry a list that lays out the steps that you have to take to follow through with a task until the customer is satisfied. Be sure to include follow up as a final step. This is particularly helpful in problem situations.

To-Do Lists - Be organized. Write down the tasks that you have to follow through and follow up on a **daily basis**. Set goals of tasks to complete every day. If you told someone that you would check back with them on Thursday then it should be on your To-Do List for Thursday. You might want to use a planner that you can note tasks in advance. Force yourself to review the list and follow through to completion.

GOOD Idea • BAD Follow Through

We all know how frustrating is it when you call a customer service center only to be disconnected after being on hold for an eternity. Recently, when I made such a call the customer service representative asked me for my telephone number. I gave it to her thinking she would use it if the call were to be disconnected. Wouldn't you know it, the call *was* disconnected in the middle of our conversation. Did she call back? **No.** I had to call her back and, wouldn't you know it, I was disconnected *again*.

After the second hang up I never called back. Do you think she even cared? Where was the follow through?

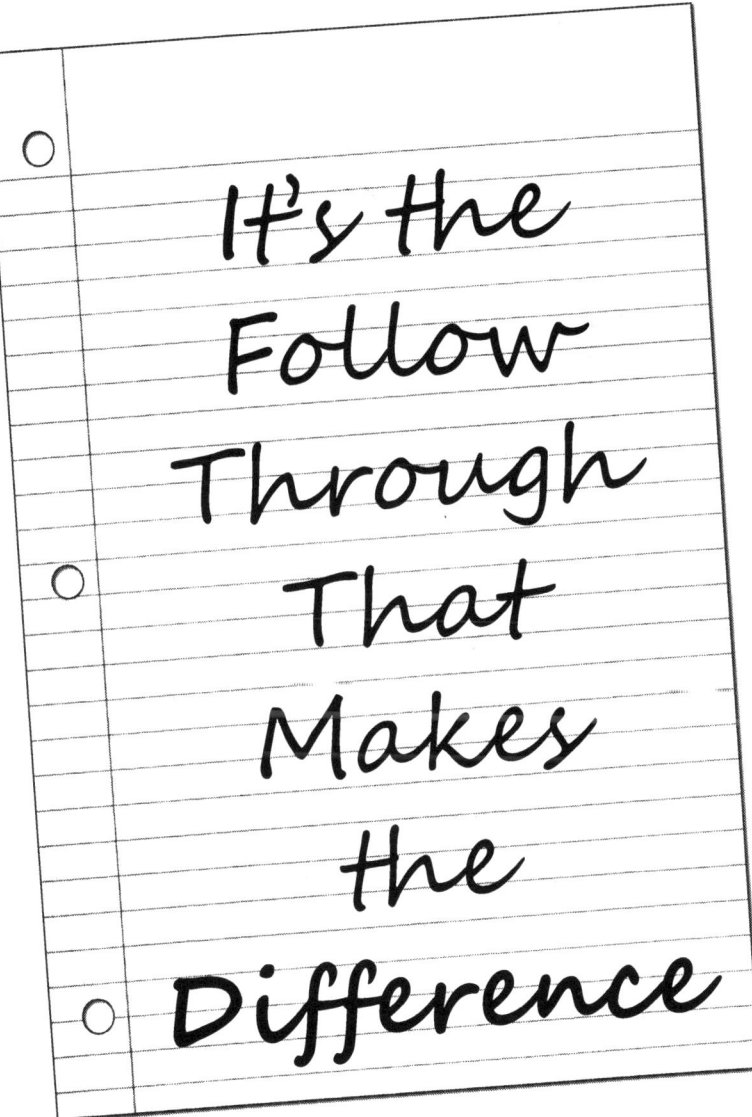

Communication Is Both Verbal & Nonverbal

www.customerserviceisfree.com

NOW SERVING 11

Communication Is FREE!

Customer service requires excellent communication to develop long standing and mutually satisfactory relationships. Communication is the *backbone* of great customer service.

You can't experience **phenomenal** customer service without communicating and interacting. Likewise, you can't offer a phenomenal experience if you don't effectively communicate with your clientele.

■■■■■■■■■■■■■■■■■■■■■■■■■■■■■
Customer Service Requires Open and Honest Communication!
■■■■■■■■■■■■■■■■■■■■■■■■■■■■■

Have you ever visited a store where no one spoke to you, where there was no communication from the employees? Not even the cashier that rang you up? It's hard to believe that this actually happens! But it does, everywhere, on a daily basis! It's this lack of communication that says one thing loud and clear, "**WE DON'T CARE!**"

Communication Is Central to Great Service

Communication is integral in every step of the customer service experience. It provides the opportunity to connect with customers on a personal level. Customers notice this, for example, when you address them by name. If the communication is effective it **humanizes** a business. From the get go you begin communicating with a greeting. It continues with respect, manners and customer recognition, all unspoken and outward forms of communication. Even apologies and listening are forms of communication. Communication can be spoken, written or posted as a sign in your establishment.

Communication Is Frequent and Everywhere!

Communication Is Cheap!

As a matter of fact, communication is **FREE**! Your customers will freely tell you what they want, what they think about your service and your product, what they like, what they don't like, and of course where you fall flat. They will provide you with the feedback that you need to improve and maintain a high level of customer service.

It is imperative that you make your customers feel comfortable talking with you about their cares and concerns or they will certainly never approach you. You need to interact with them, communicate with them, listen to them. They are your best source of constructive criticism. This can be intimidating and difficult but it's worth the challenge. Be prepared to accept the **bad** communication as well as the **good**. The bad gives you important opportunities to improve your overall quality of customer service. That's the **ultimate** goal.

TELLING COMMUNICATION

- Speech
- Tone of Voice/Attitude
- Emphasis of Certain Words
- Inflection
- Shortness, Curtness
- Talking Down/Belittling
- Choice of Words
- Being Negative
- Dodging the Answer
- Answering a Question with a Question

Good Communicators = Good Listeners

Good communicators don't listen half heartedly. They heed customers' words. They let others communicate **without interruptions** or distractions. They also take their customers' concerns to heart and show them that they really care. Good communicators are truthful and open to constructive criticism. They talk to their customers, not at them. They allow a customer to share what's really on their mind. A good communicator convinces their customers that this information is vital to continued success and improvement. This information and communication is **priceless**.

Did I Mention that Good Communicators Don't Interrupt?

Your customers will be thankful for good communication. The open dialog will make them feel comfortable, important and respected. This is especially true in problem situations. Keep in mind that many problems that arise are the direct results of **poor communication**, or a lack of communication.

Good customer service managers stay ahead of the game by keeping their staff and patrons informed. Communication is a **two-way street**.

Many people will not offer their true opinions or feelings unless they are approached about them. Many feel that it wouldn't make a difference to share it, so they never do. A customer that doesn't share their unpleasant experiences will most likely never return, yet they communicate these poor experience to others.

Talk to Your Customers

- **Interact with them**
- **Listen to them**
- **Be honest with them**

Keep the communication positive and professional. Never, under any circumstances, talk about customers, employees or even the competition in a negative light. It serves no purpose and communicates an unprofessional demeanor.

When communicating as the result of a problem, remember to be non-combative, attentive, agreeable, focused and to act with a sense of urgency. Don't become defensive. Keep those involved informed of the entire situation and communicate with the customers until the problem is resolved.

Never Argue or Disagree

Arguing only agitates customers and communicates to them that their satisfaction is not your priority. Although arguing is certainly a form of conversation, it is also the **most damaging**. One simple argument or disagreement can destroy a relationship with a customer that took years to build. Arguing should not be tolerated.

Effective Communication Is Always Truthful & Meaningful

Empty communication is an **annoyance** to customers, and, apparently, to some customer service employees. The point is, don't just go through the motions if there is no attempt to follow up on it. Don't ask if you don't want to know.

Retail store clerks routinely ask, "*Did you find everything today?*"

I once responded with a simple, "*No.*"

Funny, the clerk didn't seem to care. She changed the topic and never even blinked.

Why bother asking in the first place?

Telecommunication

Frequently phone conversations are either the very **first** time a customer communicates with a business or the very **last**. Quite often that impression isn't good. It is common for businesses to unintentionally make their customers feel like they are nothing more than a number, that their concerns are not urgent and that their time is not important.

Press [1] for English
Press [2] for Elevator Music
Press [3] to Repeat

Operators, sight unseen, are just as important to customer service as the in-store service representatives. Customers may not see their smiles, but they can *hear* them. Tone is **doubly** important on the phone. Many times a phone call is the last resort for someone that has an issue. That phone conversation could be the last opportunity to save the relationship.

- **SMILE!**
- **Listen**
- **Never Interrupt**
- **Speak Slowly & Clearly**
- **"Hold Please," is not a Greeting**
- **Call Back if you Get Disconnected**
- **Never Hang Up on a Customer**

Even with all the forms of verbal communication, one thing you may notice is that the majority of conversation is not verbal. Spoken words are just a small part of communication.

There are many other ways to communicate as well. Non verbal expressions are often more prominent and more telling than speech.

Actions Do Speak Louder Than Words

You can speak lies but you can't hide non verbal communication. Visuals play an enormous part in communication. People can see what you are saying from across the room by reading your actions, behavior and sometimes even your lips.

SEE What They SAY

- Facial Expressions, or Lack Of

- Manners/Lack of Manners

- Response Time/Sense of Urgency/Speed of Service

- Body Language/Posture (Crossed arms)

- Hand Gestures (Pointing)

- Eye Contact, Eye Rolling

- Touching (Handshakes, Hugs)

- Perceptions (Chewing Gum, Slouching)

- Clothing, Jewelry, Tattoos, Make-Up, Hairstyle

- Posted Signs or Letters

Cyber Communication

1. Respond in a Timely Manner
It is easy to overlook emails because they aren't in front of you like a customer. However, urgency is critical. Don't leave people hanging. Just like spoken comments, if a customer is taking the time to share information with you via the internet, it is important and demands your attention. I recommend responding within **24 hours**, preferably sooner.

2. Assign the Responsibilities
Designate specific people to respond to emails and social networking comments on a daily basis. Make this responsibility part of their **daily routine** (e.g. Review and respond to comments at the beginning of the day and again after lunch.) Assigning this also means that you must hold someone accountable for it as well.

3. Make a Good Impression
Send communication that is accurate and representative of your company. It could be a **first impression**. You don't want emails sent that are filled with typos and inaccuracies.

4. Personalize Emails
Avoid sending form letters. Address the situation and circumstances specifically. Attempt to obtain a telephone number so that you can communicate in a more personal manner.

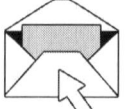 **Email is FREE!**

Consistency Creates Expectations

Consistency Is FREE!

Consistency is a common thread that runs through every successful customer service program. It is the ability to follow the same procedures, uphold the same customer service practices and maintain constant guidelines with all service transactions. It entails setting quality, quantity and service standards.

To Attain Success Employees Must Adhere to Established Standards

Consistency is necessary as customers become accustomed to a business's set standards. Customers know what to expect on each visit.

This is precisely why large chain businesses do so well. Customers know that a location in Topeka will be **consistent** with locations all across the country. They have established a reputation that policy, product and service standards will be the same.

Reputations Are Determined by Consistent Standards

If a business is consistently great then they have a great reputation. Likewise, if a business is consistently mediocre they will be known as mediocre. Inconsistent customer service is a sign of a poorly managed operation. Stability and consistency are established by **policy** and **leadership**. It is the awareness of a group of people, united, working for the same common goal which is complete customer satisfaction. You must be relentless in your pursuit of consistent customer service!

Constants Create Comfort

Customers become confident with consistencies. They know that they will have a great experience with a quality product and great customer service. When there is no consistency customers have unclear expectations.

Customers Notice

Lax or Sub-Standard Service

Customers will notice this and their expectations will be lowered for future visits.

www.customerserviceisfree.com

"Extra" Service or Product

Customers will expect more of the same the next time as well. (e.g. an extra 5% off because the sales clerk knows that you always shop there.)

Service Inconsistencies

People notice inconsistencies and will feel slighted.

- ✦ The fajitas were flaming at another table but not at mine?

- ✦ The ad stated that the sofa included free fabric protection, but I had to ask for it?

- ✦ The salon didn't wash my hair this visit even though they did last time?

■■■■■■■■■■■■■■■■■■■■■■■■■■■■■

Policies and standards become customers' expectations as a result of their past experience. Inconsistencies **lower customer expectations**, and as a result, negatively affect reputations. They are perceived as lies, unfair favoritism and possibly even discrimination.

Consistency Is Being Honest & Fair with Everyone

The public wants to do business with consistent, fair and reputable companies. Those businesses tend to **thrive**!

Businesses that constantly strive to exceed expectations are also constantly raising their own standards. Furthermore, businesses that strive to be consistent in service and product are the businesses that maintain a positive focus on the customer and the product.

Service Trumps Price

Too often businesses spend a vast amount of time and money on **managing numbers** while inconsistencies manifest in service which in turn affects profit margins which again causes them to focus even more on the bottom line. While the bottom line is obviously important in any business, it is easy to lose sight of the standards of customer service that bring the money in the door in the first place. Striving for consistency in excellent service and product will make obtaining financial goals more likely.

■■■■■■■■■■■■■■■■■■■■■■■■■■■■■

Cutting Costs Is **NOT** Always the Correct Answer

■■■■■■■■■■■■■■■■■■■■■■■■■■■■■

Focus on consistent, **superior** customer service for *every* customer.

Being consistent does not always mean keeping everything the same. A business that never changes can be quickly left behind. Businesses must advance as technology and customer habits evolve (e.g. social networking). The **mechanics** of customer service will shift from year to year, day to day and situation to situation. But, maintaining your dedication to providing superior customer service as it relates to your current standards and practices should always be the consistent factor. The goal of consistency is always customer satisfaction.

Change Is Good

Employees Notice Too

Consistency with employees is equally important to customer service. Fair enforcement of customer service regulations and the presence of dedicated authority figures provide employees with a comfortable work environment. Employees want to work for businesses that are consistent, fair and reputable.

Stellar businesses will employ stellar employees!

Are You
CONSISTENT?

We Close Early

Customers expect businesses to be open the hours posted. If a business occasionally closes 10 minutes early the expectation is that the business must close early all the time. If customers think that you may be closed they'll take their business elsewhere.

Can you afford to lose that sale?

We Don't Follow Policy

Customers don't know what your *official* policies are. They believe that everything you do adheres to company policies and that's what they expect. If you honor a promotion for an item past the expiration date today, you are setting yourself up to honor that promotion in the future. Otherwise, you run the risk of alienating and losing customers.

The manager extended the sale for a customer because she was out of town. She told her friend who then requested the same discount. She was told she could not get it.

www.customerserviceisfree.com

We Cut Corners

Businesses spend so much time developing reputations and great service procedures. Yet, so often, attention to exceptional customer service is completely disregarded and steps are compromised or altogether skipped for the sake of convenience.

"We're too busy to worry about the details."

Don't cut corners. Maintain your commitment to service standards.

We Rush Late Customers

Customers that come in later in the day are paying the same price as the people that come in earlier. Is there any reason to give them discounted service when they are paying the same amount? Do they deserve to have a sales presentation cut short because the staff is in a hurry? Late customers deserve the same experience as any other customer, even if it means working later. Every customer should be treated the same: consistently.

We Let Employees Slide

Hold employees accountable. Don't ignore the situation. You can't afford to let it slip through the cracks. "She always gives customers a little something extra without charging them. We ignore it because we are short staffed and can't cover her."

EXERCISE — Something to Talk About

How can inconsistencies impact your customers? If your service is not the same on each visit will it be noticed by your customers? Will it keep them from coming back?

Make a list of the direct results of inconsistent service. Put yourself in your customers' shoes. Look at it from their point of view. Discuss these inconsistencies with your customer service staff.

Learn from it and adjust accordingly.

Make Consistency a Priority

TOOLS of CONSISTENCY

- **Checklists**
- **Pocket Cards**
- **Training Manuals**
- **Signs**
- **Policies & Procedures**
- **Recipes or Instructions**
- **Meetings**
- **Charts & Guides**
- **Secret Shopper Programs**
- **Posters**
- **Independent Evaluations**

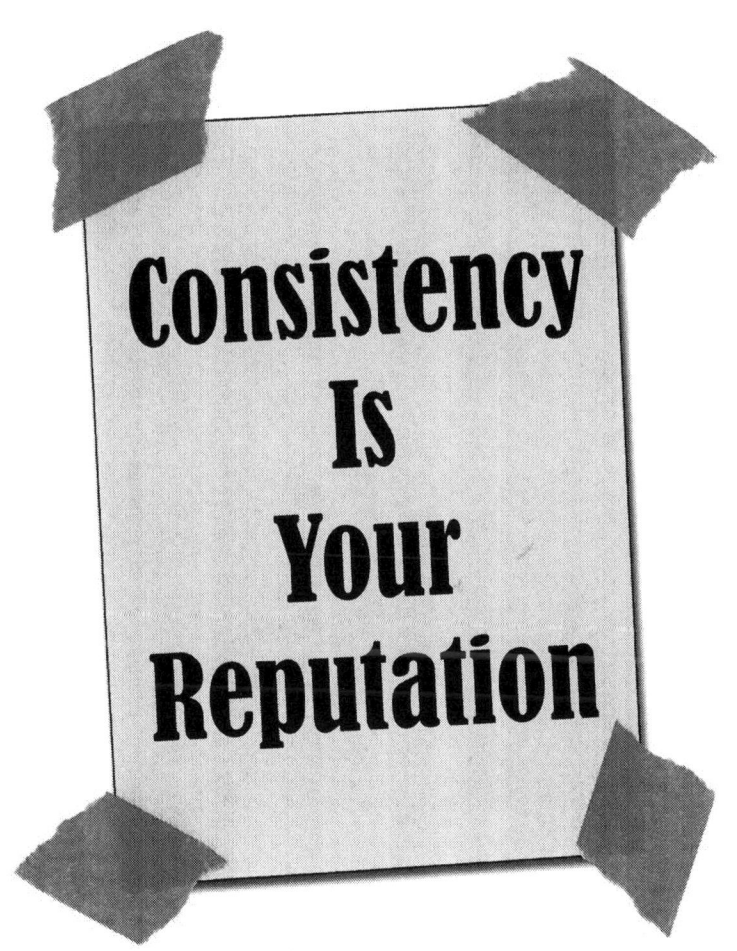

R-E-S-P-E-C-T

Find Out What It Means to Me

www.customerserviceisfree.com

Respect Is FREE!

It is more difficult for a business to earn respect than it is for an individual. People always think that businesses are "out to get them," that their only concern is the bottom line, and that customers are nothing more than a pocket book! Many businesses really do make customers feel this way. But, in reality, all any business really needs to do is show a little respect. As cliché as it may be:

■■■■■■■■■■■■■■■■■■■■■■■■■■■■

You've Got to Give **RESPECT** to Get It

■■■■■■■■■■■■■■■■■■■■■■■■■■■■

Respect is earned through exceptional customer service and it is invaluable to any business. A respected business is trusted because the standards are upheld. It's critically important for employees to **believe** in the standards and the products of a company. When employees believe the standards, they also respect them. Employees *must* respect the standards and customer service **first**. Then, and only then, will customers respect that their wishes are being met and exceeded.

Respect Builds Loyalty & Trust

Respect is a very important and complex component of customer service. In fact, you could say that respect *is* excellent customer service. Yet, respect is difficult to explain.

The Golden Rule:

Do Unto Others as You Would Have Them Do Unto You

Respect is demonstrating to people (or things) that they have value and are important to you. You genuinely care about them, their feelings and their existence. You enjoy their company and conversation. You admire them. In business relationships, respect is a display of gratitude, consideration and importance.

Businesses must **respect**, **recognize** and **appreciate** that customers can choose where to take their business.

www.customerserviceisfree.com

Establishing respect with new customers is extremely important. That **first step** is the most important step: earning their respect. The quicker you show respect to customers, the quicker you'll see the results.

Customers respect excellence, knowledge, dedication, consistency and accomplishments. Customers respect businesses or individuals that respect the community, the environment and other people. They like to see businesses involved in fundraising events, sponsoring sports teams and participating in environmental issues like recycling. These activities generate **immeasurable** amounts of respect.

Respect Is Unsolicited

Respect is the result of true selflessness. In other words, you do things because you know that they are the right thing to do, not because you expect something in return. When you treat people as if they are valuable to you (and everyone is in some capacity or another) you will in turn be treated with respect.

EARN IT!

Sincere Actions & Behaviors Derive Respect

Respectful people nurture positive relationships with customers, co-workers and employees. They treat people fairly and with importance. They realize that every person on their team, no matter their place in the authority hierarchy, has value to the common goal of customer service.

Every Person's Position Is Important

A school janitor plays an equally important part in a child's education as the teacher. A great principal acknowledges this and is respected.

Show Some RESPECT

- Listen
- Don't Interrupt
- Address People Properly
- Have a Positive Attitude
- Show Manners & Courtesy
- Tolerate Different Opinions
- Be Consistent & Fair
- Be Considerate of Others' Feelings

Principals, as well as other leaders (managers, owners, directors, etc.) are the faces of business. They portray the business' respect (or lack of it). These leaders uphold the **standards**. They appreciate and value people. They realize the significance of each and every customer and employee.

The Real Beauty of Respect Is the Associated Benefits

Effective leaders earn respect by treating and respecting all employees and co-workers equally. They also know that people will want to work more diligently to accomplish their goals if they are respected. A highly respected leader always remembers that he is only as good as the people around him.

When you are respected, people want to do more for you, they want to help you. Your competition will emulate you and your customers will speak highly of you to their acquaintances.

Likewise, your customers can also **bring you down**. We've all heard acquaintances say that they will never go back to so-and-so because they were treated poorly and disrespected.

Customers PROMOTE YOU

Once respect is lost it is nearly impossible to regain. When you lose respect, you lose business. People don't patronize places that disrespect them. It *will* be a long road to recovery.

Disrespect Customers & Your Competition Will Thank You

Disrespect will destroy a business. Don't overlook the importance of respect.

Men are respectable only as they respect.

Ralph Waldo Emerson

10 FREE
Ways for a Business to Gain Respect

1 ▶ **Community Involvement and Charity**

2 ▶ **Show & Tell People That You Value Them**

3 ▶ **Maintain Standards (Quality, Cleanliness, etc.)**

4 ▶ **Post Accomplishments, Awards and Compliments**

5 ▶ **Be Honest and Sincere**

6 ▶ **Respect the Environment - Be Green!**

7 ▶ **Acknowledge Others' Opinions and Ideas**

8 ▶ **Mind Your Manners (Ladies First, Open Doors, etc.)**

9 ▶ **Appreciate Your Competition**

10 ▶ **Empathize with Your Customers and Employees**

CHECK YOUR RESPECT

Use this short true and false assessment to evaluate your level of respect. Be completely honest with yourself and your answers. Consider your interactions will all people, personal and professional.

True False

☐ ☐ I listen and allow people to speak *uninterrupted*.

☐ ☐ I treat *all* people with a sense of worth.

☐ ☐ I use manners and common courtesy.

☐ ☐ I do not talk down to or about others.

☐ ☐ I consider others' feelings.

☐ ☐ I uphold and believe in standards and policy.

☐ ☐ I treat people fairly.

☐ ☐ I am selfless when dealing with others.

☐ ☐ I have a positive attitude.

☐ ☐ I accept that others' opinions may differ from mine.

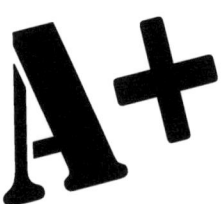

If you did not answer true to all of the above statements, you're not alone. You have some areas that you can improve in, as most people do.

Each statement will literally cost you nothing to adhere to. **Start today!**

Find a **FREE** printable version of this respect assessment on our website, www.customerserviceisfree.com.

RESPECT:

Even Though It's FREE We Still Have to Earn It

It's Ironic that *Paying* Compliments Is

Compliments Are FREE!

NOW SERVING 14

We love to be complimented because it makes us feel good. We all love to hear that our hair looks great, our children are adorable and that our work efforts are noticed and praised.

A Simple Compliment Goes a Long Way!

Compliments are the whole reason that we go through the trouble to wear trendy clothing, drive nice cars, eat at the best restaurants and go the extra mile at work to make a lasting impression. There is great pride in knowing that others approve of what we choose and do. Everyone wants to be noticed and it is always nice to hear it!

However, compliments are quite rare in our stress-filled, fast-paced, profit-obsessed daily lives. When we do receive them, they are unexpected. Most people are pleasantly surprised to receive any recognition, let alone a selfless and genuine compliment.

It's often downright shocking!

Compliments Complement Customer Service

Compliments are a great addition to exceptional customer service because they help to establish new personal business relationships and strengthen existing ones. More importantly, compliments are cordial ice breakers that put people at ease.

Compliments say, "I notice you. I want to talk to you." They are individual and personal. They break down communication barriers, generate positive energy and can even lower stress levels. They help to make a human **connection** and put all parties involved on the same level. They show that you care about the customer experience, service and satisfaction.

People **Radiate** with Smiles When You Pay Them Compliments

TRY IT!

Compliment the next five people that you come into contact with. Even a simple remark of admiration will do (e.g. "I really admire your confidence.") What did they do? They smiled. They straightened up. They made eye contact. You got their attention. Paying a compliment helped make a personal connection. It developed an instant opportunity for you to create a conversation and a relationship. It opened the door, so to speak.

Avoid **back-handed** compliments, especially when complimenting employees. "I love the way that you communicate with customers. **BUT** ... you really need to limit the amount of time you spend with them." People learn the routine and come to expect the "but." The compliment and the constructive criticism may be valid points, but neither has the intended impact when presented together. They should be addressed separately to maximize the positive power of the compliment, as well as to stress the importance of the suggestion for improved customer service.

Expect the "But"

Give compliments **freely**, but be honest about it. When you aren't completely honest you come across as over zealous and patronizing, even fake.

Avoid sweet-talking and buttering up your customers. You want compliments to be natural, not forced. Don't sugar coat it.

Sincerity Is of the Essence

The giver must truly believe in the compliments they share in order for them to have meaningful impact for both the giver and the receiver.

Compliments Require Awareness

Being specific and insightful with your compliments shows that you are paying attention, that you see the details. **"Good job!"** is a statement. "I appreciate your attention to detail in the presentation charts at the sales meeting today," is a compliment.

Share Compliments

www.customerserviceisfree.com

Compliments Told in the Presence of Others Are Magnified

If there is one thing that people like more than compliments, it's knowing that other people are aware that they were complimented. "The boss said my sales were higher than everyone else's sales."

A Public Pat on the Back Is a Great Confidence Builder

Post compliment letters, emails, awards or any other complimentary communication where customers and employees can view them. Remember that everyone loves to be appreciated, acknowledged and complimented.

Customer service employees are often **overlooked** even though they are our direct link to the public. It's in your best interest to pay them compliments. They will feel valuable and appreciated, which will make them better suited to provide an excellent customer service experience.

Kudos Worth Giving Are Kudos Worth Sharing!

Daily Compliment Goals

EXERCISE

Select a number of compliments that you want to share. Start small and increase the number as the time goes on. Go out of your way to share compliments with people that you normally would not. You will see an instant change in attitude. It's a positive change that you can almost feel in the air. At the end of the day jot down your successes. Eventually, if you stick to your goals, you'll **exceed** your number without even trying.

When receiving a compliment it is professional and courteous to offer a simple smile and a heartfelt *"Thank You."* It is actually impolite and inconsiderate to dismiss or make light of it.

www.customerserviceisfree.com

Honesty Is FREE!

Honesty is the cornerstone of exceptional customer service. If you had only one policy, it would have to be honesty.

One Dishonest Person Can Destroy the Image of a Business

All companies are founded on principles of truth and have the customer's best interest in mind. Honesty is the key factor for all business policies. Rules, guidelines, manuals, training guides and the like are established to keep employees **honest** and true to the beliefs, morals and standards of the business. Companies always have honest intentions, however, people and employees do not.

For instance, **dishonest employees** steal diamonds out of customer's rings. Jewelry stores do not. Many large companies have closed because of the dishonorable actions of one individual.

Hold Customer Service Staff Accountable

Managers should be involved and **aware** of the quality of customer interaction.

Keep the Employees Honest

Customer Is King

Leaders need to spend time in their stores, show rooms, restaurants, offices and hotels. Nothing can compare to true, honest observation and interaction between employees and customers. It keeps customer service employees and managers on their toes and honest to the company's core values.

An honest business must be sincere with their actions as well as their words.

It's ironic that many businesses proclaim "**Customer Satisfaction is Our #1 Concern**." All across America, people see customer service slogans and mission statements plastered on the walls above the checkouts while cashiers unenthusiastically snatch money out of their hands. It's a sad reality. Be honest with yourself, is customer service really your top priority? Those sayings on the wall don't hold an ounce of truth if there isn't an attempt to implement them. Your actions speak louder than words.

Customers show businesses their appreciation by patronizing the stores that offer honest value, services and products. An honest business is one that can be trusted; trusted to treat customers respectfully, to charge fair prices, to provide value, to be truthful in their quest for satisfaction, to be genuine and show sincere appreciation to everyone.

Honest-to-goodness business owners, managers and customer service personnel are earnest and act with heartfelt concern for their patrons and their patrons' interests.

Have Honorable Intentions & Principles

Being honest requires making conscientious decisions, free from deceit, that will benefit the long term relationships of customer service.

Walk in Your Customers' Shoes & Put Their Needs and Experiences **FIRST**

Your first reaction might not be the best when you take a step back and look at the big picture. **Ask yourself:**

What will benefit the customer in the long run and make them leave satisfied and want to return?

Honesty means being forthright and telling the truth. Don't try to cover up mistakes either. People *always* see through it. They may not see it right away but it will catch up with you sooner or later. **Fess up** and correct the problem so that you can move forward. Be sincere. It is easy, and quite obvious, to spot when people go over-the-top and create dramatic schemes and stories. Stick to the facts. Get to the point. Don't embellish. Being truthful when mistakes happen is far more valuable than trying to hide it.

The Public Values Honesty

Often your best customers become so as a result of problems being handled honestly & satisfactorily.

In fact, resolving problems with honesty diffuses anger and frustration. It calms people and puts them on a level playing field. Honesty creates a personal connection filled with emotions and genuine concern for their customer satisfaction. It's so much more than a heartless apology that's forced and dishonest.

Your Customers Will See the Truth

www.customerserviceisfree.com

Dishonesty & Deception Do Not Pay

A business may be able to "**pull one over**" on a few people, but the results will be devastating when those customers find out. Marketing tactics have become so rampant with mistruths and deception that our first reaction is "What's the catch?" or "It's too good to be true?"

- A sandwich shop runs an ad offering *all* sandwiches for just $5. However, there is a small disclaimer that excludes several "premium" sandwiches. So which is it? Are ALL sandwiches $5 or not?

- A computer store sells a computer with a video card that is different than the one listed on the website. Honest mistake?

- A promotional item is advertised as 100% **FREE**! But the order form requires that you to pay for over inflated shipping and handling charges.

- The telephone company is offering unlimited calling for just $69.99. The small print, however, states that it is only valid to new customers.

These methods are not totally honest, to say the least. They are misleading and will break down the trust that is so important for any business to get. Is it worth alienating and losing customers over?

Nobody Likes Being Deceived

Why do you think a business involved in fraud is so quick to collapse? Fraud exposes the lack of honesty in a business.

Customers will immediately seek out alternate businesses if they feel that they are not being treated fairly and honestly.

www.customerserviceisfree.com

An
Honest Business
is a
Successful Business

We Trust Honest Businesses

Honest businesses make good faith efforts and are always forthright in their business practices. They realize the value of being trustworthy. Their honesty is paid back to them by loyal people who appreciate that their interests are considered.

FREE
Word-Of-Mouth Advertising

Loyal people spread the word and promote businesses that are honest and trustworthy.

That's the most valuable thing that any business could wish for!

LITTLE WHITE LIES

Little white lies are **harmless** fibs that are nothing more than incidental mistruths. They have no real impact on anyone, right? In business, little white lies are told to avoid embarrassment, pacify customers or to hide mistakes.

> **The customer doesn't have to know!**

Do you tell a customer that a problem was a supplier's fault when, in reality, your team made the error? Is it acceptable to blame someone else for a mistake that you made so you don't have to face the truth? Do you say you lost the work order when you never even wrote one up?

To a customer, it makes no difference *who* made the mistake. What matters is that the mistake was made in the first place. In customer service, "the company" made the mistake and "the company" is the one that suffers the consequences. It serves no purpose to place blame by telling little white lies.

One huge problem is knowing when you've gone too far.

Where do you draw the line?

How far will employees go with "harmless" lies? How do you train your customer service staff to be truthful? A little white lie to one person, is not necessarily a little white lie to another. Everyone has different judgments and morals. The more you lie the more that lies are told. They snowball out of control. Before you know it, everything gets "resolved" with a lie.

A **lie** is a **lie**, but **truth** is **trust**!

Lies hurt your business. Lies break down trust. **Tell the truth instead.** Use the truth to your advantage. People appreciate honesty. The value that is derived from sincerely addressing the situation and the opportunity that it provides you is far greater than any little white lie could bring.

Something to Talk About

Brainstorm and have an honest discussion about honesty in your workplace.

Why is it important? What harm is there in telling "little white lies?"

Honestly, it Pays to be Honest!

101 FREE THINGS
You Can Do NOW to Improve Service

1 • SMILE!
2 • Teach Employees to Smile
3 • Say "Hello!"
4 • Thank **EVERY** Customer
5 • Make Eye Contact
6 • Praise Employees That Smile
7 • Learn Customers' Names
8 • Address Customers By Name
9 • Send "Thank You" Emails
10 • Follow Through & Complete Tasks
11 • Never Walk In Front of Customers
12 • Present Employee Awards
13 • Post Compliment Letters & Emails
14 • Share 5 Compliments Every Day
15 • Apologize When You Make a Mistake
16 • Listen to Your Customers
17 • Listen to Your Employees
18 • Lead By Example
19 • Show Passion for Customer Service
20 • Seek Out Opinions

- **21** • Make Lasting First Impressions
- **22** • Return Phone Calls Promptly
- **23** • Don't Lie
- **24** • Don't Argue with Customers
- **25** • Mind Your Manners
- **26** • Observe Your Customer Service Staff
- **27** • Hire People That Smile
- **28** • Constantly Find Ways to Improve Service
- **29** • Learn What the Competition Says About You
- **30** • Don't Blame Others
- **31** • Invite Customers to a Focus Group
- **32** • Treat Employees Fairly & Consistently
- **33** • **WOW** Your Customers
- **34** • Hand Write Notes of Appreciation
- **35** • Don't Accept Mediocrity
- **36** • Be Aware of the Big Picture
- **37** • Choose to Have a Positive Attitude
- **38** • Address ALL Problems
- **39** • Hold Employees Accountable
- **40** • Act with a Sense of Urgency

41 • Keep Customers Informed
42 • Talk Positively About Your Competition
43 • Keep Your Promises
44 • Be Aware That Customers See *Everything*
45 • Don't Use Profanity
46 • Smile When You Talk on the Phone
47 • Seek Out Problems to Resolve
48 • Never Answer with "I Don't Know"
49 • Don't Speak Negatively About Customers
50 • Don't Answer the Phone with "Hold Please"
51 • Don't Interrupt
52 • Reply to Emails Promptly
53 • Maintain Standards & Policies
54 • Don't Cut Corners
55 • Use Checklists & Manuals
56 • Appreciate the Importance of Respect
57 • Consider Others' Feelings
58 • Accept Differences in Opinion
59 • Treat All People with a Sense of Worth
60 • Don't Talk Down to People

61 • Greet Every Customer Immediately
62 • Teach Everyone to be a Greeter
63 • Walk In Your Customers' Shoes
64 • Offer Firm, Confident Handshakes
65 • Share Clients' Names with All Employees
66 • Treat Others as You Want to be Treated
67 • Accept That Mistakes Happen
68 • Follow Through then Follow Up
69 • Don't Delegate Customer Satisfaction
70 • Observe Customers' Body Language
71 • Search the Internet to Gauge Opinions
72 • Develop Customer Service Listening Plans
73 • Treat Each Customer as Your Only Customer
74 • Create Positive Experiences for Everyone
75 • Anticipate Customers' Needs
76 • Show Enthusiasm for Customer Service
77 • Don't Judge Customers by Appearances
78 • Ban Staff Smoking In Front of Your Business
79 • Do One Thing Every Day to Improve Service
80 • Acknowledge Good Service When You See It

81 • Make Customer Service a Priority
82 • Involve Management in All Problems
83 • Learn from Mistakes, Take Corrective Action
84 • Don't Ask if you Aren't Prepared to Respond
85 • Strive for Consistency
86 • Train Employees Not to Congregate
87 • Evaluate Your Staff
88 • Address Poor Service Issues
89 • Accept That Clients Choose Where to Shop
90 • Brainstorm for Ways to Improve Service
91 • Replace Poor Customer Service Staff
92 • Require Employees to Dress Appropriately
93 • Provide Feedback to Employees Regularly
94 • Interact with Customers
95 • Call Back if You Get Disconnected
96 • Dote on Customers' Kids
97 • Admit When You Are Wrong
98 • Focus on Details
99 • Be Mindful of Perceptions
100• Be Ready to Go Above & Beyond

#101

Train Customer Service

EVERY DAY

Without FAIL

www.customerserviceisfree.com

BRAINSTORM
with your staff and add more to the list!
Send your ideas to: ideas@customerserviceisfree.com

102 • _____

103 • _____

104 • _____

105 • _____

106 • _____

107 • _____

108 • _____

109 • _____

110 • _____

See,

Customer Service Really Is
FREE

Customer service can **make** or **break** a business. Excellent customer service will make you stand out in a crowd and give you a leg up on your competition.

> **Excellent Customer Service is an ONGOING Endeavor**

Customer service requires a passion for customer satisfaction and a commitment to training your staff **every day**. You can't just pass out handbooks and hope that everything falls into place.

Excellent customer service includes finding people with great attitudes, smiles, manners, honesty and the ability to communicate and listen effectively. It entails sharing memorable greetings, compliments and thanks. It means being consistent and respectful as well as knowing and admitting when you are wrong. Customer service also requires following through to ensure customer satisfaction. Customer recognition and the **WOW** factor are the icing on the cake that can *really* set you apart and differentiate you from your competition.

The best part about customer service is that it is **FREE** to give *and* **FREE** to receive. It simply requires the dedication and effort to demand and hold your people accountable.

There's no sense in wasting money on elaborate and expensive marketing plans if you ignore customer service.

Focus on Customer Service

Not only will you **save money** on marketing, but you will make more money! Satisfied customers will promote you with **FREE** word-of-mouth advertising to bring you plenty of additional business.

Customer Service Is FREE!

Thank you

for Making the Commitment to Improve Customer Service

■ ■ ■ ■ ■

Be sure to visit
www.customerserviceisfree.com
for **FREE** printable awards,
worksheets, signs and more.

Plus, get useful tips, reader stories,
practical advice and the **FREE**
Customer Service is FREE monthly newsletter.

■ ■ ■ ■ ■

Send comments, suggestions, questions
and experiences to

info@customerserviceisfree.com

www.customerserviceisfree.com

Excellence in Customer Service is worthy of recognition. Present Customer Service Awards to commend stellar performers and recognize their commitment to satisfying customers and the success of your business.

Find a **FREE** printable version of the Customer Service Award on our website, www.customerserviceisfree.com.

Customer Service Is FREE

Proof

Made in the USA
Charleston, SC
22 December 2010